To Jay —
thanks for being there!
In Poems,
Sandy

Working Hard for the Money

America's Working Poor in Stories, Poems, and Photos

Edited by
Mary E. Weems & Larry Smith

Working Lives Series
Bottom Dog Press
Huron, Ohio

Bottom Dog Press
P.O. Box 425
Huron, Ohio 44839
Lsmithdog@aol.com
http://members.aol.com/lsmithdog/bottomdog

Our books may be ordered direct or through
Small Press Distribution at SPDBooks.org
or Baker & Taylor Books.

Acknowledgements
[See Page 2003 for permissions.]

Cover Art and Design
Jim Lang

Book Design
Larry Smith & Mary E. Weems

Assistant Editor
Jennifer L. Miller

Our special thanks goes to Marcus Williamson
for his continued support of our work.

We thank the Ohio Arts Council
for its continuing support.

Ohio Arts Council

CONTENTS

Section IV: Life On The Streets

Section V: Disabled List

© Photo by Jim Lang

Classism: The Germination of this Book
by *Mary Weems* and Larry Smith

> "In America, the harder the work is, the less the pay."
> - Robert, homeless temp worker

❑ **31,139,000 U. S. citizens live in poverty; 11.3% of the population; 22 % of Blacks and Hispanics live in poverty; 30% of single mothers with children live in poverty; 16.2% of children under 18 live in poverty (U.S.Census 2000). 1 in 6 people living in rural America lives in poverty (Center for Budget and Policy, 1992).**

❑ *One of the reasons major social tragedies,like the long term poverty that exists in America, continue to receive so little mainstream media attention is that the general public becomes accustomed to their reduction to numbers as in the above eye opening statistics. While there are a few economic success stories in my family including some who own businesses, the overwhelming majority of my large, close-knit family is included in the 22% of Blacks in poverty and they all have names; and lives spent from birth to death on the margins of America, un-college educated, with little or no time for dreams between swing and second shifts, between jobs, between living from pay-to-pay making sure that rent, food, and clothing are secure.*

I hope that this book, this collection of work by and about the millions of poor working-class folks in this country, who cross all race, religious, and cultural backgrounds will help our reading audience add images of people to this reality. That it will encourage them to become active participants in both acknowledging, respecting, and reducing the number of poor working-class and homeless Americans. - Mary

❑ I remember that when I first heard the term "underclass," I felt physically ill. It was an involuntary response–physical, mental, and emotional–to what I took as a term of degradation...the "under" class. I have long seen that there is a class system in this country, despite a commercial move to make us all part of the "consumer" class. It's an aspect of our society that plagues those who would deny it. You can't help a problem if you refuse to see it. Class exists in America, despite the larger egalitarian realization that we are "all just people." We are "just people," but we don't really treat each other as such. When I sought to discuss this elsewhere, I tried to make a pie diagram of the classes in America and could not escape the ranking language that labels "upper," "middle," "lower," and now "under" class. It reminds me of elementary school where we are grouped by reading abilities. Mine was based on airplanes and I was among the "piper cubs," a step above the "helicopters," but a long way from the "jets." And so people are always being "classed" in this country, especially in our schools. What we do with this awareness is crucial. We could choose to deal with it—face it—come to understand it, and maybe get out from "under" it. I drew my pie diagram with equal shares for value, but I could not escape the judgmental language. - Larry

❏ **The Poverty Level for a family of 3 in the U.S. is $13,700, so that a person can work full-time at the minimum wage and still officially be living in poverty. In many poor neighborhoods, consumers find that they are charged retail prices as much as 49% higher for groceries that are low in fresh produce and meats. (*Newsweek* Feb. 24, 1992).**

❏ *Yes, "You can't help a problem if you refuse to see it," and for many of us who float between the lines of the bottom and the middle, focusing on the plight of those less fortunate than we are is painful and often avoided. I believe that it's not that the powerful, and privileged are refusing to see it—they have spent the last several centuries building the poor working class poverty base that is an essential element of capitalism, making the homeless invisible, and being poor a crime the victims commit on themselves.*

I didn't hear the term underclass until I was a graduate student, but I've always known that whatever the current buzz word was—Black people in America were at the bottom of the list. Once you get past the under and poor qualifiers, the terms middle and upper class have to be color coded, because when white folks talk about middle and upper class and give the dollar minimums, they leave most people of color out of the conversation; because what most of us earn doesn't come anywhere close to the figures quoted.

*I have lived in the ghettos of Cleveland all my life, and have owned a home less than 10 minutes from the rundown and now torn down, roach invested row apartments I was born in for over 20 years. In my neighborhood, you can mark the houses lived in by their owners by the way the property is maintained. The rental property is falling down, the owned property is well kempt. Black people who represent 99.9% of the population, do **not** own most of the businesses. The prices are so high, the quality of merchandise so low, the stores so dirty and drastically different from comparable businesses in white neighborhoods* *that when I want to shop I have to travel. I cannot buy skim milk, fresh produce, bread, or meat in my neighborhood, and this is the way it's been all of my life - Mary*

❏At a writing conference in Albany, New York, I chaired a panel of "working-class writers." Each had some fine things to say about what class meant to them and how it affected their writing as work. As a writer and publisher of working-class writing, I declared our noble goals of inclusion. So when we moved into the question and answer period, I was struck by two responses. First a beautiful dark woman stood up and declared, "I need to say something about your idea of work ethic. I am Puerto Rican, and, believe me, my people know work, but they also have been abused by work for centuries. Work can be noble, but it often is used to enslave people." I drew a breath on that. I had been expounding on "working-class values" and extolling the "doing a good job" ethic of most workers. Yet I knew she was right, just as I knew the drudgery and oppression surrounding the work of my own family of steel mill workers. I too am conflicted about work as it is used in America. For, while I feel "home again" driving into the smokey Ohio River Valley, I also know there is a cost to the land and the people in that laboring. Work should not be idealized. The second awakening came from a young man in a heavy jacket. He rose from his seat to declare, "Hey, I want you all to know that I've been excluded from all your talk. I'm homeless, have been for two years, but I'm a writer and I work as much as I can. Where do I belong in your talk of working-class? Where do the poor?" I felt a pressure in my chest. How had I been so blind? How strong was this classist conditioning? Though I grew up working-class on the edge of poverty, had I come to exclude those who couldn't or didn't work, or those who worked and could barely subsist? I wanted to revise some of the anthologies we had done. I wanted to broaden our definitions to include those without jobs or support, those who had been excluded too long. This was something I knew and even understood, but I hadn't yet lived or realized.   -Larry

❏ **Since 1970, there has been a 178% increase in the number of involuntary part-time workers in the U.S. (*U.S. News and World Report*). 1/3 of the homeless in this country are children; 1/3 have mental or physical health problems. (U. S. Census 2000).**

❏ *As a descendant of slaves, as the granddaughter of maternal grandparents who worked as stock "girl," maid, porter, and janitor, and dealt with the in-your-face humility of racism everyday of their lives; as the daughter of a single-parent, with a tenth grade education who* *wore out her carpal tunnel hands running the macaroni/baked apple machine at Stouffer's; as the member of a family who's **always** had people on the edge without jobs or support, me included, I've always realized and understood being "excluded too long."*

The distinction that I share with Larry is that while I've worked for low pay, and spent a short time on welfare when I was between jobs and without the benefit of child support, I have never done back breaking, boring, spirit-killing work. Hating and avoiding school after high school graduation, but raised to value education, my first job as a teenager was at the local library and all of my subsequent employment until I earned my graduate degrees has been in business and university offices. The day I walked across the stage to receive my Ph.D. in education, the first on either side of my family, I felt light and heavy at the same time: light with the joy of accomplishment, heavy with the load of unfulfilled family dreams strapped to my back.   - Mary

❏ I remember my friend Bill Wright's story about an incident at a protest march for America's Poor a decade ago. "We had boarded the bus in Cleveland and driven to D.C. with a group of people from the area homeless shelter. It was a good ride and we got to know each other along the way and hear each other's stories." Bill was drawn to one young woman who slept in her coat and woke to look out across the snowy landscape. "When we got to D.C. we were told to use the restrooms and come back to the bus in an hour to assemble for the 7 mile march to the Capitol. As the young woman stepped off, I went up to her and said, 'Listen, be careful where you go. Don't get lost.' She looked down at the street then smiled up at me and said, 'It doesn't really matter. I'm lost wherever I am.'" That was a decade ago at a time when we thought universal health care would be coming for all. Today, we don't even raise the issue. And yet at the back of my head and deep in my heart is the admonition of Senator Hubert Humphrey that a nation should and would ultimately be judged by how it treated its poor. I had lived through President Lyndon Johnson's War on Poverty. I had seen enough of America, its potential and its suffering to become uneasy with denial. Who would speak for those who had no power?   - Larry

The make-a-difference answer to Larry's question is as many of the currently powerless that are aided in becoming empowered. One of the main goals of any human rescue mission is to help those in need until they are able to help themselves. As the work in this book makes as clear as fresh well water—the powerless have much to say, and no one else can say it as they can   - Mary

❑ **The number of people (under 65) living without any healthcare in the U. S. is 44,000,000 or 16% of our total population. (U. S. Census 2000).**

❑ I began teaching in 1971 at a branch or community college with a diverse population, most of whom worked. I watched many struggle with whether they belonged in college. One woman was on welfare, with five children; she had been homeless for a time, even served a little time in jail, yet she was here now in this school that was there to help her and all others. She graduated a few years ago with a bachelor's degree in social work, but the road wasn't easy. Gradually I learned that, as person and teacher, I held the keys to some of their doors, that I could work to accept and not exclude those who would enter. I've found that t is easier to give inclusion than to win it from others, and giving it tears down walls for us all. Though I had always written of my working-class roots, I now saw them as the primary material of my life and work. I developed courses in it, wrote articles on it, through Bottom Dog Press published the working-class writings of others. In creating alternatives, we all give more room to breathe and move around in. - Larry

❑ *As someone who's been the only recently-African face in more college courses than I care to remember, inclusion has a special significance. Before I developed the level of self-confidence, positive identity and self-love I have today, I spent years holding my breath, struggling for room to breathe, waiting to exhale -Mary*

❑ **The telling photo images of the Farm Service Administration:** Dorthea Lange, Walker Evans, Ben Shan, Paul Strand, and others who have followed them. **The powerful films that tell this story...**_The Grapes of Wrath, Meet John Doe, Sullivan's Travels, Salt of the Earth, Raisin in the Sun, Norma Rae, Matewan, American Dream, Silkwood, Roger and Me, My Family, Harlem Diary, The Long Walk Home, The Doll Maker,_ and others.

❑ **The long legacy of writing about the downtrodden in America: The Prose–** Rebecca Harding Davis, Theodore Dreiser, Sherwood Anderson, Anzia Yeziarska, Willa Cather, Mike Gold, Grace Lumpkin, Jack Conroy, Agnes Smedley, Edward Dahnberg, Meridel Le Sueur, Tillie Olsen, Zora Neal Hurston, James T. Farrell, John Steinbeck, William Saroyan, Grace Paley, Jack Kerouac; more contemporary: Russell Banks, John Sayles, Toni Cade Bambara, Alice Walker, Toni Morrison, Gloria Naylor, Dorothy Allison, Sandra Cisneros, Barbara Kingsolver, and others.

The Poetry– Walt Whitman, Carl Sandburg, Kenneth Patchen, Muriel Rukeyser, Kenneth Fearing, Genevieve Taggard, Nikki Giovanni, Allen Ginsberg, Bob Kaufman, Gregory Corso, James Wright, more contemporary: Lucille Clifton, Marge Piercy, Joy Harjo, Sue Doro, Philip Levine, Antler, Jim Daniels, Tess Galla gher, Raymond Carver, June Jordan, Chris Llewellyn, Mary Fell, Gary Soto, Maggie Anderson, David Budbill, and others.

❏ At a Working-Class Studies Conference, Youngstown State University, July 2000, Dan Kerr, from Case Western Reserve University, presented a community action program that works with the homeless temporary workers of the Cleveland area who are "basically being kept in homeless shelters as warehouses for cheap labor." The pay is poor, the work irregular, fees are charged for equipment and transportation, there are no health benefits, no hope of going on full-time, real risks to life and limb, long days at minimal wage. The temp agency keeps half of their pay. The companies that hire them are not just mills and factories, but stadiums, museums, and schools. Our economy is based on slave wages; it works off the backs of our poorest. Finally, Dan introduces two temp workers. Robert rises, smiles, and stares into the crowd. "I don't have a college degree, but I'll tell you what I've learned, folks. In America, the harder the work is, the less the pay." -Larry

❏ *Dan Kerr's comment encapsulates what for me is the central message of the writings in this book. Poor, and formerly poor, and the children of poor working-class writers repeat this in the interviews, stories, and poems in different ways over and over like a powerful, all-consuming chant. In cities all over Americia, people are underpaid, humiliated, abused, injured, and discarded based on their lack of formal education or training. They pick the crops, deplete the mines, clean the homes, landscape the yards—serve, serve, serve often invisible to the millions who benefit from their labor. As Nelson Demery, III asserts in his poem "My Parents: Snoring" I work for the day when its time to "[w]hisper now/a new song/of callused hands at rest/may their sleep be a peaceful slumber/may they never dream of scrubbing."The backs of the poorest are about to break and when they do, when they atlas shrug the weight of the world what will happen? What will the well-to-do do next?*

One of my favorite poems in this collection, for its freshness of language, use of metaphor, and its political statement about waste and wealth is Mac Lojowsky's "The Coming Revolution." I envision the

work in this anthology, and in the other writings of poor working -
class people all over America beginning a socio-economic revolution.
A revolution of words that prompt action. Words that spark feelings,
memories, conversations, economic and socio-political game plans,
and the kinds of changes that will move America toward real freedom,
equity, and opportunity for all of its citizens including the homeless.
 - Mary

❏ And so, in coming to this book on America's working poor, Bottom Dog Press opens its eyes and heart to a real world of struggle and quiet strength. These are writings that witness and participate. The lives may be those of the writers or projections of the lives of others they know, but in all cases they are personal and involved in the world they describe. The character of the life they describe is authentic and valued by the writer.

The hope in this book lies in our individual and shared ability to feel empathy for these lives of our sisters and brothers. As novelist Barbara Kingsolver declares, " I believe the creation of empathy is a political act. The ability to understand and really feel for people who are different from ourselves– that's a world-changing event. It's the antidote to bigotry and spiritual mean ness, and all the terrible things those deficiencies lead us into" The editors and the skilled writers and photographers assembled here believe this and so bear witness for us all.

                    - Larry Smith & Mary E. Weems
                    (August 2002)

Long Story   **Maggie Anderson**

I need to tell you that I live in a small town
in West Virginia you would not know about.
It is one of the places I think of as home.
When I go for a walk, I take my basset hound
whose sad eyes and ungainliness always draw
a crowd of children. She tolerates anything
that seems to be affection, so she lets the kids
put scarves and ski caps on her head
until she starts to resemble the women who have to dress
from rummage sales in poverty's mismatched polyester.

The dog and I trail the creek bank with the kids,
past clapboard row houses with Christmas seals
pasted to the windows as decoration.
Inside, television glows around the vinyl chairs
and curled linoleum, and we watch someone old
perambulating to the kitchen on a shiny walker.
Up the hill in town, two stores have been
boarded up beside the youth center and miners
with amputated limbs are loitering outside
the Heart and Hand. They wear Cat diesel caps
and spit into the street. The wind
carries on, whining through the alleys,
rustling down the sidewalks, agitating
leaves, and circling the courthouse steps
past the toothless Field sisters who lean
against the flagpole holding paper bags
of chestnuts they bring to town to sell.

History is one long story of what happened to us,
and its rhythms are local dialect and anecdote.
In West Virginia a good story takes awhile,
and if it has people in it, you have to swear
that it is true. I tell the kids the one about
my Uncle Craig who saw the mountain move
so quickly and so certainly that it made the sun
stand in a different aspect to his little town
until it rearranged itself and settled down again.
This was his favorite story. When he got old,
he mixed it up with baseball games, his shift boss
pushing scabs through a picket line, the Masons

in white aprons at a funeral, but he remembered
everything that ever happened, and he knew how far
he lived from anywhere you would have heard of.

Anything that happens here has a lot of versions,
how to get from here to Logan twenty different ways.
The kids tell me convoluted country stories
full of snuff and bracken, about how long
they sat quiet in the deer blind with their fathers
waiting for the ten-point buck that got away.
They like to talk about the weather,
how the wind we're walking in means rain,
how the flood pushed cattle fifteen miles downriver.

These kids know mines like they know hound dogs
and how the sirens blow when something's wrong.
They know the blast and the stories, how
the grown-ups drop whatever they are doing
to get out there. Story is shaped
by sound, and it structures what we know.
They told me this and three of them
swore it was true, so I'll tell you
even though I know you do not know
this place, or how tight and dark the hills
pull in around the river and the railroad.

I'll say it as the children spoke it,
in the flat voice of my people:
down in Boone County, they sealed up
forty miners in a fire. The men who had come
to help tried and tried to get down to them,
but it was a big fire and there was danger,
so they had to turn around
and shovel them back in. All night long
they stood outside with useless picks and axes
in their hands, just staring at the drift mouth.
Here's the thing: what the sound must have been,
all those fire trucks and ambulances, the sirens,
and the women crying and screaming out
the names of their buried ones, who must have
called back up to them from deep inside
the burning mountain, right up to the end.

Part One

The Coming Revolution

© Photo by Fred Lonidier

How the Poor Are Kept Poor   **Larry Smith**

"The harder the work/ the less the pay."
-Robert, temp worker

In the shelter you are bed down,
though the bunks are close and hard.
No good to bitch or complain,
your lot to bear and learn from.
The women and children live in a
another building. You can understand that.

Up at five, you don't see them again till night
when you return from work to
stand in line at Trinity Kitchen.
So you go over to Ameri-Temp to beg for a job,
sign in and wait for a chance to work.
Old donuts and coffee is breakfast
while you sit along the wall.
You bring a book but hide it
when the job-hustlers arrive.

Sometimes they don't even look at the list.
It's "You...and you...and you...and you...
and you...and you" though it doesn't hurt
to be young and white.
The rules are just for you:
"Don't look poor. Don't come in drunk.
Don't question anything."
When you enter there's a mirror and sign:
"Would you hire this person?"

So you try to look eager and strong,
ready to work the jobs that can cost you a finger
send fumes into your face, asphalt into your lungs.
The only healthcare is what you give yourself.
The safety gloves and glasses come out of your pay.
You pay for the ride out, and just hope it'll be there
to drive you back, or you'll have to walk into town,
maybe catch a quick escort out from a cop.

Besides the factory, warehouse, and stadium work,

there's the cleaning, tossing trash,
picking vegetables in a hot field,
the stripping and grinding,
sanding and painting, the digging and lifting.
If you turn down a job, you fall off the lists forever.
"That's why they call it work," they grin and spit
beside your shoes. You give them all you've got,
bring home twenty-four bucks for 8 hours work.
Something to spend, something to save up,
only they don't like that.

You want to get out, get your own place, a regular job,
only you can't save up the rent and deposit
or hide your parole status.
And you can never get your 90 days in,
even when you're the best at the job.
You sit on your bench or stand at your machine
knowing: You are the "quick labor,"
kept in the warehouses of America's back streets.
You are "the labor ready" our economy requires,
and this is how the poor are kept poor.

© Photo by Jim Lang

Title Panel for Exhibit of Photos and Interviews   Fred Lonidier
WELFARE IS POOR RELIEF

"As the true foundation of riches and power is the number of working poor, every rational proposal for the augmentation of them merits our regard." —Jonas Hanway (18th century philanthropist)

Oil shortages, inflation, and rising unemployment have left American voters receptive to a war on welfare. In the 1960s and early 1970s, an unreflective, though brand new, assumption led to an optimistic assessment of America's future. Permanent economic growth would fuel continuous prosperity and provide the resources to absorb and resolve social problems with neither conflict nor sacrifice. This faith in the benefits of unlimited growth underpinned national policy, the emergence of a counterculture, and the relatively relaxed attitude toward the expansion of social welfare. However, in 1973, the oil embargo neatly sliced the underpinnings away from assumptions of permanent abundance, and individuals' difficulty simply finding gasoline for their automobiles became emblematic of the new task confronting families: maintaining—not expanding—a standard of living. As inflation and unemployment followed the energy crisis, the resumption of buoyant growth became increasingly evanescent, and, everywhere, ordinary people reverted to an older psychology of scarcity, now tinged by the anxiety and resentment that accompanies downward mobility and, particularly, in America, the fear that their struggles and sacrifices will not insure a better life for their children. In the search for scapegoats and ways to trim public expenses that followed predictably, welfare and its clients, especially its black clients, were inevitable and early targets, displacing attention from the falling profits and return on investments that, even before the first oil crisis, had signaled the end of unlimited growth.
(Michael B. Katz, *In the Shadow of the Poor House*).

In reality, American capitalism is going through one of its most decadent and anarchistic periods in history. In the age of Reagan Republicans and neo-Reagan Democrats, any form of rational and democratic planning is attacked as violating free enterprise, while the inherently anti-social tendencies of corporations are now out of control. Working people are suffering as profitable plants are closed in pursuit of even greater profits, as the captains of industry become captains of megamergers, paper transactions, and the heralded transition to the "information and service economy" —captains of destroying our nation's industrial infrastructure.
(Eric Mann, "Keeping the GM Van Nuys Open," in *Labor Research Review #9, Labor Tackles the Local Economy: Reindustrialization from*

Below, Midwest Center for Labor Research, vol. V, no. 2 Chicago, Il, 1986)

First, when mass unemployment leads to outbreaks of turmoil, relief programs are ordinarily initiated or expanded to absorb and control enough of the unemployed to restore order; then, as turbulence subsidies, the relief system contracts, expelling those who are needed to populate the labor market... Some of the aged, the disabled, the insane, and others who are of no use as workers are left on the relief rolls, and their treatment is so degrading and punitive as to instill in the laboring masses a fear of the fate that awaits them should they relax into beggary and pauperism.
(Frances Fox Piven & Richard A. Cloward, *Regulating the Poor: The Functions of Public Welfare,* Vintage Books, NY,1971).

"I sit on a man's back, choking him and making him carry me, and yet assure myself and others that I am very sorry for him and wish to lighten his load by all possible means—except by getting off his back."
—Lev Tolstoi

Interview with Veteran, Teamster,   **Fred Lonidier**
Homeless Student

My name is Julian Flores Jr. and I'm living in the beautiful streets of San Diego. I'm a Vietnam era veteran who served in Latin America. But being they trained me to be a professional soldier, I can survive on the fat of our city. But I hate to beg, but sometimes you have to to survive.

About forty-five percent of the bums on skid-row are Vietnam Veterans that have given up and won't move any further than skid-row because they've gotten tired of getting doors slammed in their face.
They've gotten tired of coming to school with no income and me, you need a pair of big ones to stay in school with no income and keep your curriculum up without being put on probation and things like that.

My goal here is [a] social welfare [degree] right now, so I can work in the field. I want to be a psychologist, a combat specialist psychologist to help these Vietnam Veterans that are in the street that people cannot relate to.

It will take me approximately a total of about another five years to get the degrees I need. And it's going to be a long, hard five years, but I'm going to do it with the help of the government or mother nature and I'll depend on mother nature because the government is not dependable whatsoever: only for their own raises and their own benefits.

But for the people, they're not here for the people no more. They're just out there for the almightly green dollar.

My curriculum should be completed if I don't let the way I'm living get me down. Like living in the bush, going to the missions and eating, bathing when I can and accepting the weather, whether it rains or not.

Last semester I was living in the rain and I don't think there's too many students that have done that. But I know there's other Vietnam Veterans that are coming to school with no income also.

And you want to ask where to drink a coke-a-cola and you can't because you can't afford it and it's embarrassing.
You're older than most of the students here anyhow, so it's still embarrassing, but I'm still a leader.
I have a lot of people that follow me and respect me and they know how I'm living and what I'm doing.

I've worked but for very minimal wages. I can't raise a family here in San Diego on $3.35 an hour.

I've tried and I won't go home to see my family because I can't even afford to buy my son a gift.

And I'm an American and I'm proud to be an American.

I have a son. He's ten. I have a wife that lives in Logan Heights below poverty standards and I haven't had any opportunity to go down there to visit because I'm not cleaned up. When I get cleaned up, I'll go down and get an opportunity to see my son.

So, I did a good justice for my country and now my country is doing me an injustice by not hiring me in any type of agency, even as a janitor.

I left my family back around 1980/81. That's when I was last with my family and now it's me and God. I can't support my family, so I don't have the right to see my family. If I had this income, I would be more than glad to see my family. I did have a drinking problem and I didn't think it was a drinking problem until later in life.

A few years later I realized that I did have a drinking problem since the service. I thought all Americans should drink and that's not the way it is because we weren't born with a Budweiser in our mouths. I was led astray by American advertisement and by all these macho images they've got on t.v. and theaters. Everybody's drinking and if they told the public they were drinking tea instead of booze, everybody would be drinking tea instead of booze, but now I don't drink...

My "ex" [gets VA support] only for my son which is approximately about eighty dollars a month. She's working minimum wage jobs and they've pulled her from jobs; the I.N.S. have pulled her out of jobs. They've transported her from other spots of the area because she looks like me, but she's legal and they will not give her any kind of legal papers.

I've been fighting Immigration and Naturalization Services for over seven to ten years and I still can't get any assistance from I.N.S. I can't get no green card for my wife.

Dishwashing, construction, warehouse work, truck driving, odd jobs that were lucrative. But, being who I am, I couldn't get the right pay. A civilian would come in that never had any military and they'd give them two or three dollars more an hour than myself. But I was a work horse. I was born and raised an American and we like to work. We like to earn our way and they haven't given me the opportunity to earn my way and that's all I'm looking for is an opportunity to earn my own way. They won't give it to me.

I was a Teamster in San Francisco for eleven years and then I came to San Diego. The union that I belonged to was called Local 860 Warehouse, affiliated with the Teamsters in San Francisco. I've gotten fired many a times but I've gotten re-hired because they were trying to unjustifiably fire me for a dirty shirt or something ignorant.
But the union saw it was ignorant and protected my job. The thing is that the people that say they're against unions are usually people that are well-to-do. They like to pay $3.35 an hour and make more money and laugh at the people who work their dogs off. But unions are the best thing that I have ever run into in my life.

Homeless Student © Fred Lonidier

Interview with Machinst   **Fred Londiner**

We were laid off in, let's see, like March of '83; and that was for thirteen weeks. That's like cutting it pretty slim. I was bringing home $400 plus a week. Now I am getting $166 and all my bills are jamming up and they are giving me red notices on this and that, so I try to borrow whatever I can. I have a saving plan coming in...I guess, in October of over five or six grand. It's kinda touch-and-go until that comes. We're OK so far, but if I can make it until the savings come in, it'll be OK. But if they go much longer, it gets real tough. Like the car is broken down now. I have no funds to get that fixed so in the mean time I'm "mister bicycle rider!" In the 97 degrees, yes.

I was supposed to receive my Unemployment check this past Friday. And I called yesterday, which was Monday, and they said they would contact me again today. Well, I didn't wait for that to happen. I jumped on the bicycle over this morning to avoid the sweltering heat. I got down there and they didn't know where my check was and they suggest I ride back up and go to the local post office, which I did, and they didn't know either. They had me fill out some forms down there and they said they'll get back to me. I got back home and sat down and the phone rang, and they said they had the check down at Unemployment and they've just received it, that the mail just got there.

So I jumped on mister bicycle and pedal my little fanny back on down there. It was about noon Mr. Beads-of-sweat dripping off Mr. Forehead. I got the check and went over to the bank, deposit it; cover some of my bounced checks and rode back here and drank about a quart of Kool-Aid. Which meant it comes out of my pores.
Yeah, that was a fun day. Well, what happened, I noticed on the check, was they fail to put my apartment number on there, and the way they delivered the mail here, they have a bunch of boxes with everybody's apartment numbers on there and all I had was just the address. So there is 180 units here so they just sent it back. They didn't want to try to guess. They had my apartment number to begin with, they just fail to put it on it. It was on the first check I received. I made sure they correct it. I didn't feel like doing that again.

You feel worthless, definitely. The first thing, you still wake up early in the morning and go out and make a few bids on places to get a job and come back and you kinda get tuned into the television and after a couple of weeks you just get squirmy and just don't feel like you're worth a shit.

You're a little irritated. I've overcome that now. I sort of snap at the children there a little bit and I caught myself. So I take a walk and calm myself down. But it's just a sort of an empty feeling. I feel sort of self-conscious when I walk out there. I see all the house mothers going, "What's this guy doing walking around in the afternoon? Well the old man doesn't work." It feels kind of humiliating walking in using Food Stamps whereas I used to be able to walk in there and slap the buck down.
But I'm glad I have them. It's just a kind of an anxious feeling, that's basically it. Either empty or nervous type.

Sleeping in, this isn't the same. You lay there and you worry about what problem might come up in the future. It's sort of like Murphy's Law, whatever can go wrong, will, and it seems like it everyday. The car, bad checks. It's a circle of things. It's really exercising my patience and my will to be calm and safe with a bunch of troubled water.

Just had this baby here in May, end of May. Got laid off at the beginning of July. It wasn't very good timing. One of the supervisors said, "I know it's kinda tough you just had another kid." I said, "Yeh, right." Can't even have a heart. That little girl is too. She is almost three months.

There is one poor guy, he just bought himself a house and he was just scraping by on the payments. I don't know how he is doing. He just had a kid himself, got two kids. It makes things rough. If you don't have anybody you can....

If I couldn't get in touch with her relatives for short-time loans or something. Our phone is supposed to be shut off the 21st of August. Then the gas and electric, I guess, start at the end of this month. I try to save the Unemployment so I can pay the rent here for September. So, without any help, we're sunk.

I've known a lot of people who have been on Unemployment and if they live by themselves, they didn't have a family, it seems like it's pretty easy. Well, not really easy, but a lot easier than with a family because you're always worrying about taking care of the crew. I have been on my own a lot of time and I could live on just a couple of beans or something but...

The families that have been on Unemployment that I have seen, been a lot of disharmony in the household. The wife is frustrated. Doesn't have enough food for the kids and the husband feels like a crumb and he's trying to get a job and come home and they fight and it's a real ugly situation. That's not good. Not good when you're used to a certain level of living and just got the rug pulled out. You have gotta be strong to be able to pull through the whole thing. I don't know anybody that can. I can't. We have flare-ups here but try to keep it to a minimum but it just tears the family apart.

I know a lot of people on Welfare. Like I said, right now we're getting the food stuff. That's a shot away from it. It makes me feel kinda less a person and I like to be out doing something and bringing the check home.
Better than just being a number waiting in line and get dolled out by the little portion for the month and, "You'd better not mis-spend it," and this and that. It's sorta like...you know I get food in my belly and everything but it sort of saps my spirit.

I know a lot of people on welfare that...I see a lot of people that get into a rut. They get on it, they get used to it. Like filling out the form is nothing. They just do it and sent it in, get the money and become couch potatoes. Get highly involved in the "soaps" and booze it up.
It's just a day to day thing and you just grow old that way. That's ugly to me, I don't like that, but if push comes to shove, for family, I would do that if I couldn't find employment anywhere. I wouldn't want to do that.

If you don't have the skill and you are cut-off from a job that's dwindling and you don't have any opportunity for another skill then it's gonna put you right at the mercy of the government. And the government don't want you. They'd rather have everybody out working. But they cut the program, and then cut the spending and so that cuts down on the job and they don't have any training thing.

It's sorta a circle there. There's a lot of guys that work that had their wives work also. Sorta envious on that. They're putting down for houses and everything and I am trying to get the rent paid.

Interview with Work-Study Student   Fred Lonidier

I know that she [mother] had Food Stamps. I don't know all the facts really clearly, just what I have remembered. I think also that she sort of didn't like it. I think she was always a little embarrassed. She didn't openly hide everything because when we were going to the store, she had Food Stamps. So I always felt it was kind of embarrassing. But I think she had Welfare's regular checks and she had Food Stamps and Medi-Cal.

She worked as a waitress. I think she only got it when she wasn't making barely any money. Because for a while she was working as a cocktail waitress and she made plenty of money. And then she always thought that she was rich then. I think she only got it when she had to.

She has this unpleasant situation and she doesn't like to think about it. She doesn't like to deal with it. She always does it only when she absolutely has to because she hates going there. She said...the people there are very unpleasant and they make you feel bad about yourself.

I went with my mom once to the Unemployment Office and that wasn't very fun at all. It was awful.
It's just grouchy, mean ladies that don't want to see you there, don't like what they are doing and...,I don't know, they are just unpleasant to you.

There is a lot of people there. Sometimes you worry whether it's really worth it. I think we waited in line for forty minutes or something. It was a few hours,I think. It's such a drag.I guess that's what they want...They are successful. Something you definitely want to stay away from. Which, I guess, that's what they want. Because I saw a lot of mothers with little kids going there and you know their mother will say, "Oh no, we'll have to go do this." And the kids learn that's something they want to stay away from.

Well, they figure out your need and then they give you 100 percent of your need with loans and Work Study and then grant. I have a loan, a guaranteed student loan and I have...,I am not sure what the grant is called, and I have Work Study.

They tell you at your preliminary [meeting] what they think you are going to get, and three forms later it's different from what they think you are going to get and I don't know why. I don't know whether, it's just, they just don't tell you everything or whether they just make it complicated or...I don't know what it is but it seems kind of a game to me. I don't do enough research myself too.Because I don't read everything they give me in detail. I just look it over. That's probably one of the reasons why I don't understand it all. It seems like they just give you piles and piles of papers.

I haven't had any problem but I am used to living without any money so I guess that's what they've figured too.People with financial aid are used to living without money. I know because I have a lot of friends that aren't on financial aid and they live differently than I do. N. has a car and Ntl. is making a lot more money than I do. Well, I have my bike.

I've always felt like I am one of the poor kids, not one of the rich kids and I kind of, I know I have a bias against rich people...So in a way it's a "minority" feeling. Because they say minority is financially disabled or disadvantaged.

It's a kind of a shrinking, a little bit, feeling. I never hide the fact either. I tell people I'm on financial aid. But if I think about that, it does feel like I should be a kind of shrinking away a little bit.

But I don't know exactly why either because I don't hide the fact. I think it's just society. You're not supposed to be as good if you are poor. Because, for some reason, you haven't worked up to the success philosophy. Your family hasn't...because, I guess, of society.

You are supposed to be able to become successful if you work hard enough and successful means you...it's a stereotype because I don't feel that way. But the feeling takes over anyway no matter how hard you try to fight it. Since that's how most people think.

It's crazy because I have five classes and two jobs and no time. I don't know, especially if you pick a hard major. I mean it would be a lot easier if you pick an easier major. You don't have to take as many classes and they're not as hard classes. I know some people do that, but sometimes you're just insane.

Well, they have a lot more time to study.

It's harder, I mean, I guess working...I think also, working is good when you're in school because then you already have some experience [than] when you're not in school so it might be a lot easier to get a job. But on the other hand if your grade point average isn't as good... I worry a lot about which to put more time into: my work or more time into school. Because your grade point average matters also for getting a job. But it's really hard to tell which will be better. It's hard being in competition in classes with people that you know have a lot more time to study. A lot harder when you have roommates that want to go out to dinner....

I found that really hard because if you don't have money to go out to dinner, and that's what everybody is doing, you just have to say "I don't have the money," and either they go without you or they don't go. But usually they just go.

I shouldn't have to work now if I am going to work for the rest of my life. And I should concentrate on school since this is the time I am in school.

The money has to do with the parents because that is what your financial aid is based on. Because most of my friends, their parents paid for their college. They get checks from the mail from their parents every month and it's a lot more than I get from financial aid.

I think the school is particularly rich. I mean it's La Jolla too and it's very expensive to live here. It's disgusting. There is a lot of money. That just means a lot of poor people aren't here too. Almost everybody I know has a car, and then usually they have nice cars. Their own stereos, their own cars, a lot of clothes. I mean a lot of clothes. Most of them are pretty conservative too, politically. I don't know, I am biased too. So it would all be negative.

My roommate, when she moved in, she had three fourths more stuff than I did. I am just the person who doesn't have a lot of things...Because I move so many times that I know I don't like to carry around a lot.
I don't have anything, really. I don't have any furniture. We moved into the apartment, all of the furniture is hers...beds and she had a whole living-room set. I think it's just they have whatever they need, whatever they want. They go clothes shopping a lot.That's a big thing. Piles and piles of clothes. Going out to dinner is not anything special either.

I guess going skiing is no big deal and flying places is no big deal. If I go somewhere it's always get a ride from the "ride board." So that's a lot different. They can just drive their cars. They can go...They can just go. That too is a big problem, just going home I have to find rides and cannot go home when I want to and they can do that whenever they want to. They can drive wherever they want to and if I need a ride it's always a problem. They have to like you well enough to...be there at certain times. It's really difficult although the boyfriends I have had in college have liked me well enough, even though there are so many different things that I have to do that [dating] could only be one of them. But, I mean, in eating out, that's when you get to go out to dinner. That's when they are paying for you to go out to dinner and the movie. Because I wouldn't be going out to dinner if I didn't have a boyfriend most likely at all.

The other boyfriends I've had weren't [poor]...they've always had plenty of money and cars and things but the boyfriend I just had graduated and he was on Work Study and he had the same family situation I had. But he graduated and he has a job. So he knew. He could understand everything that I am going through because he'd already been through it and he had the same hard classes that I had so he is very understanding.

I don't know whether it's just me having a bias or not. Rich people don't have the same view and the same problem and they just don't understand where you're coming from. It's not a concern because they don't have to deal with it. Whenever they need money, it's there.
They never have to think about it because it's always there and it's nothing to worry about. It's not an extra worry. All their worries are with school and other things. This is not theirs so they just don't think about it. They don't think about the other people who do have to worry about that. I think there is also something that (I don't know if it's common) ...my roommate...I know she resents me for being on financial aid.

I don't have to ask my friends for money anymore. Plus she doesn't know what it's like to live with the family without any money too. So she doesn't know that's what is involved in the Work Study at all.
I know she just thinks that it's free money that I get from school. And I think she thinks that it's my choice to be so busy too, and she resents me for not being around for her too. Not having as much fun for her too.

Work and Its Malcontents   Ben Satterfield

In an article titled "Work and Its Malcontents,"*The American Scholar*'s Joseph Epstein quotes his father's advice: "If you work for a man for a dollar an hour, always give that man at least a dollar and a quarter of effort." Epstein, without meaning to and completely against his intent, identifies the chief economic problem in America, that employers in general *expect* to get more than they give fair value for because working people have been taught to give more to their jobs than their paychecks will ever realize. *"At least,"* Epstein's father urged, implying that a dollar and a half of effort for a dollar's pay would be preferable, and two dollars of effort would be praiseworthy. I suppose there's no end to how much more the worker should give for nothing—the more the better.

Along with millions of others, I received the same sort of pernicious advice when I was young, and I always thought, "That's great for the employer, but what about me? Am I not in effect undervaluing myself?" The older generation, apparently believing the lies of Horatio Alger, Jr. and other shills of the profit system, seemed to look at work solely from the owner's standpoint, never from the worker's (The employers in this country used to control morality, and, as one might expect, the slave morality persisted). I thought then and I think now that the advice I got was worse than wrong; it was wrong-headed and treacherous. We are now seeing the disastrous results of this national dupery.

That work is a matter of giving and not taking is an ingrained belief in this culture which affects people at all levels but most of all those at the bottom of the pay scales. The poor are least able to do anything about the conditions of their employment, so they have to keep giving, but middle-class workers, most of whom are trapped in a kind of wage slavery that is growing more constricting every year, are affected as well. I noticed when I worked for a bureaucracy in California that employees could give without stint—come in early, stay late, work through their lunch hours and in general devote as much extra time to their jobs (without additional pay) as they could—but if anyone tried to take off early or extend a lunch period, that person could expect an "admonishment" from a supervisor, who never mentioned all the extra time freely given to the job; that was expected. This one-way-only attitude is found throughout America, and, whether acknowledged or not, surely adds to worker discontent. When employers talk about "give and take," I interpret their meaning is that the employee gives and the company takes. Since most people need their jobs and are in no position to take a stand or to fight against injustice, the imbalance is likely to continue throughout America—and will certainly continue for the poor, who are helpless to combat the forces that dominate their lives. Companies are simply not discerning about the effects of their actions; they are so accustomed to operating from a position of power that they too often mistake might for right.

The attitude that workers should give more than justly required is widespread covering the country like a dense fog, clouding our vision and hiding the truth. People naturally repeat what they have been taught, and if they are indoctrinated with ideas that work against their own best interests, they will strain to find ways to justify their beliefs rather than challenge the teachings. Epstein tells of his father complaining about a man he employed for fifteen years who showed up on time every morning: "You would think that once, just once he would be early." The employee's conscientious effort was not enough, his reliability and punctuality remarkable—attributes that were unappreciated—only made the employer resent the fact that he wasn't getting more than he was paying for.

This country prospered as a result of slavery, which in essence is getting more from labor than the employer pays for, and economically speaking we haven't gotten away from the slave model. Business, industry, and government (BIG) are the massas and the rest of us perform more or less to their liking: they call the tune we dance to and we are expected to continue dancing even without the music. We are, in truth, expected to love the song of labor and believe in it, to *whistle the massa's happy tune*. Of course, the best way to keep slaves contentedly in line is to get them to participate in their own enslavement, to get them to believe in the system that exploits them. Capitalism needs a slave class (poor working people are truly in bondage), the more desperate the better.

"The concept of people's duty to work," Bertrand Russell wrote in 1935, "has been a means used by the holders of power to induce others to live for the interest of their masters rather than for their own." The holders of power (the BIG leaders) have been amazingly successful in the past, but signs are beginning to point to the end of their crippling control. Angry voices of protest are growing stronger and louder, and attitudes are slowly changing. At the end of the '80s, Tom Bender declared, "The imposition of work upon people in ways that are boring, stultifying, or nerve-wracking is criminal." Yes, the word he used was *criminal*.

Garbage has to be picked up, shelves have to be stocked, offices have to be cleaned, sewers have to be kept clear, and so on. Many jobs are dull, repetitive and stupifyingly boring, but they must be done, and the people who do them are the young, the poor, and the desperate, those who have no choice if they want any income. The young usually move on to better jobs as they complete their schooling or receive promotions; they are able to tolerate awful work because they view it as temporary and see the future as providing chances for deliverance: they rightly expect to have a choice.

Poor people, a growing class (according to the Census Bureau, 19 percent of workers earned low wages in 1979, whereas 26 percent did in 1990), are always without choice, and middleclass workers in the Reagan-Bush protracted recession began to get a sample of what the poor must endure on a regular basis—and they became embittered by this dose of economic woe.

Today, income is worth less than it was ten years ago or even five years ago, and the average workers, like treadmill runners, have to keep trotting, not to get ahead—the promise of the American Dream—but to avoid losing more ground (This generation, according to economist Robert Solow, may be the first in American history to leave its children poorer than itself). They feel powerless to control their finances and angry that a wasteful government keeps sticking them with the bills for its mistakes—the half trillion dollar S&L bailout, for example—and for the support of the rich. Companies keep raising prices without any corresponding increase in wages, and business in general seems concerned only with "the bottom line," which, in case anyone is unaware, indicates the all-coveted *profit.*

During the fraudulent "energy crisis" of 1973 oil companies raised their prices immediately when OPEC asserted itself (Any increase in the cost of crude oil would naturally take months to be reflected in prices at the pump, but the oil companies—*all* of them—saw opportunity in adversity and uniformly opted to make economic matters worse for the country but better for themselves; their year-end profits were so enormous, so obscenely high that Congress woke up long enough to conduct one of its useless "probes," but, unsurprisingly, did nothing constructive). When oil prices rise, the prices of goods in general go up because of increased transportation costs. At least, that's what we're told, and it seems reasonable. However, when oil prices fall, consumer prices do not decrease, despite the fact that transportation costs are drastically reduced. It's another one-way-only relationship. During the oil glut in the '80s, gasoline prices dropped about 40 percent at the pump, but inflation continued its climb unfazed by this fact.

Business truly believes in *taking* but not *giving.* Every summer during the peak vacation period, gas prices are pushed up exploitatively to fatten the bottom line.

U.S. Department of Agriculture records indicate that in 1994 the average price of a hog dropped 30 percent while the retail price of pork declined only 3 percent. Another and better example: several years ago, the peanut farmers had poor crops, and to keep the growers from suffering economic loss, prices were raised so that meager yields brought just as much money as previously bountiful ones had. As everyone knows, the price of peanut butter zoomed up—and it keeps rising even now. Good crops of peanuts do not result in lower prices or any break for the consumer. For American business, opportunity for profit is not to be missed regardless of the effect on the economy or the future CEOs are lavishly rewarded for their ability to gouge the consumer, whom they view as help-less. People at the top keep taking; for them rape equals reap.

"Since 1980 the price of virtually every source of energy, every agricultural commodity, every one of the earth' s minerals, and every forest product has declined," claims Stephen Moore in *The Public Interest* (Winter 1992). Yet prices keep rising unchecked, whereas hourly wages and job benefits, according to the Economic Policy Institute, have declined since 1980 by nearly 10 percent and 14 percent respectively. Average workers give more as they get less.

Book publishers, knowing that a 360 page book often sells for the sane amount as a 180 page one, maintain that their prices are high because the cost of paper has skyrocketed, but they are merely adopting the well recognized stance of "passing the buck." In business it's always the other fellow's fault. ("Over the past decade, the real price of paper," claims Steven Moore, "fell by 10 percent.") But if the cost of paper were cut in half tomorrow, would book prices drop? No. The CEOs might get fat bonuses to add to their hyperinflated salaries, but you are still going to dig deep at the bookstore, you are going to have to give more.

Professional economists, who would like us to believe that their shell game is too complicated for general comprehension, continually speculate about the cause or causes of inflation, unable to agree among themselves or even to identify the problem, but there is only one cause and it's obvious: *greed*. It is greed that motivates, and opportunism that satisfies greed? and ruins the economy and hurts you and me—but it's part of the system. In the fall of 1983, Hormel announced its intent to cut hourly wages from $10.69 to $8.25 despite reported profits of nearly $30 million. Hormel showed no consideration for the very people who had helped it make so much profit (Barbara Kopple's award winning documentary film, *American Dream*, records the human damage done by such greed). Although the average pay of the American corporate chairman exceeds that of the average worker by a ratio of nearly 100 to 1, we're constantly told that these executives are more interested in the challenge than the money. Time Warner chairman Steve Ross, the highest paid CEO in 1990, received a compensation package totaling $78 million the same year his company laid off more than 600 employees, whose total earnings amounted to about one-third of the CEO's pay. What a challenge!

In 1992 the highest paid American executive was the appropriately named Thomas First, Jr., CEO of the Hospital Corporation of America, who grabbed $127 million in salary and stock-options. He was left behind in 1993 by Walt Disney CEO Michael Eisner, whose $203 million salary broke a record. The rake-off by greed-heads at the top is unabashed: the June 27, 1994 issue of *Time* magazine reported the median total compensation (salary, bonus, and incentive grants) earned the previous year "by the CEOs of a representative cross section of Standard & Poor's 500 companies" was $2,291,000. This excess began and flourished in the '80s, an era of "trickle down" economics that rationalized unbridled avarice and ignored its consequences. Chrysler chairman Lee Iococca, defending the more than $20 million he made in salary, bonuses and stock options in 1986, declared: "That's the American way. If little kids don't aspire to make money like I did, what the hell good is this country?" Drug dealers can say the same thing, and be just as proud of their results.

Behind the greed and opportunism is the accepted notion that the employer should get more from the ordinary workers than he gives just pay for, and this economic apostles' creed has been generally supported by Americans of all classes—by those who suffer the most from it—and seldom challenged. As a nation we have been brainwashed into docility, and are suffering because of our reluctance to question, to challenge, to *think* rather than mouth platitudes that were created by the massas to serve their own interests.

Those platitudes are destroying us.

Most of us are taught to believe in the American Dream of material success. We are taught to believe that there is dignity in work and that exemplary effort will be rewarded, while all around us we see evidence to the contrary, evidence that can no longer be ignored or rationalized away. We are frustrated that our dollars are worth less and that we have to work harder merely to *maintain* our standard of living, not improve it. As our disposable income shrinks, the government prepares to tax us even more, leaving the prosperous and wealthy alone, letting business do whatever it wants, and—as usual—ignoring the poor, who are always the first to suffer and who must bear the heaviest burden. How much more can we give to those who only want to take?

Work, which has forever been the bane of the poor, is becoming the scourge of the middle class, who are growing resentful and starting to feel like suckers in an elaborate con game that manipulates the human need for value and self-respect. The workplace is spawning a rapidly growing number of malcontents who are beginning to see that there is no honor in endless giving. If work had some intrinsic dignity, we would be able to recognize it, since most of us have to work, and we wouldn't need the sermons that apologists such as Epstein keep raining on us like commercials for the American Dream. My early work experience, which may be similar to that of thousands of others, taught me nothing about the so-called dignity of labor or the value of giving extra effort for no reward (I should say "pay" because "reward" is too grand a word for the pittance I received for the unleavened drudgery I performed), but it did teach me something about exploitation. My first job was on a farm in Georgia and it was mind-stunning, body-wracking labor: chopping cotton, corn, and other crops, picking cotton and harvesting watermelons. This "grunt work," which was necessary, was demeaning to the body and diminishing to the spirit, I thought, and completely lacking in any dignity. Furthermore, the landowner would drive by periodically to check on his fieldworkers, and he wanted to find everyone stooped and toiling in the blistering heat. That is a perfect picture of capitalism: the owner in a comfortable car watching the workers perform back-wrecking labor for a few cents an hour. And it is a picture that stays with me.

The first job I got with a social security number was as a grocery clerk in an A&P, a relatively clean and easy job compared with farm work. All the Atlantic & Pacific employees were paid on Saturday nights, and the store manager, who was a deacon in the Baptist church, gave us cash, whose receipt we acknowledged with our signatures in a record book. Every Saturday night the manager would indicate where I was to sign in the ledger for my pay, keeping his hand on the page with one finger pointing while I signed, his hand obscuring the payroll data. But one Saturday night—I like to think it was my last—I managed a peek at the figures and discovered that I was on the books for more money than I was getting. The manager, of course, was pocketing the difference. That incident has become symbolic and stays with me, too, since it is a perfect example of the middleman's willingness to step on and cheat those below him. It also shows hypocrisy and the power of self-interest, both of which capitalism promotes.

Another job I had as a young man—I am using my experiences, which are not unusual, to show how workers become malcontents—was that of stevedore: pure labor. I had to join the appropriate union before the company would hire me, so I joined and paid regular dues, hoping that the union could protect me from overexploitation at least. It couldn't. One Saturday morning, after I finished work at 8 a.m., the manager, another middleman, told me that I could work a shift that day for regular pay (Saturday work was supposed to receive double pay). When I told him I wanted what the union contract required the company to pay, he told me to go home, knowing that I needed the money. Like the church deacon, he was more than willing to step on those under him, to gouge and cheat for his own benefit. I could have worked that day, received standard pay, then complained to the union—even though I had reason to doubt the union's willingness to defend me. But let's say the union might have been willing to file a grievance on my behalf, what good would have been accomplished? Thereafter I would have been a marked man, a troublemaker who would always be assigned the most agonizing jobs and denied any extra work—and probably fired at the first opportunity. As things were, I merely kept working without hope of overtime pay or anything else until I was "let go" for a reason I no longer remember. I do remember that I was expected to *give*, and my unwillingness to do so numbered my days.

To help prepare myself for a career, I took a night school class in the late 60s, when I had a white collar job that I loathed but kept because it was the best available and I had to support myself and my wife and help support children. In this class were mostly blue collar workers who wanted to improve their station, but who had no concept of elevation other than that provided by the organizations for which they worked. During breaks they would discuss the propaganda they absorbed from listening to an ultraconservative radio program sponsored by the multi-billionaire H. L. Hunt, a reactionary whose interests were opposite to their own. Yet they swallowed his cant in hungry gulps, believing in the American Dream as they toiled and sweated for a system that worked against them. I was amazed that they voted for the very politicians who would rob them in favor of the rich and ardently supported a system that exploited them for the benefit of those who have never cared about much of anything except profit. Without question these same people displayed flags of patriotism and offered their sons to be slaughtered on foreign land in an immoral war that benefited only the military-industrial complex (the BIG). The system works! It really does, but it needs a lot of bodies, a lot of unquestioning slaves.

"Everyone but an idiot knows that the lower classes must be kept poor, or they will never be industrious," said Arthur Young, and what is worse, he was serious. The middle class has been deceived into thinking of the poor as their albatross—not the rich, the true enemy—and the poor have been so long maligned that they accept the stigma of their position as deserved. I marvel at how thoroughly the rich have conditioned the poor and the middle class, at how skillfully they have manipulated attitudes, controlled loyalties and channeled desires to serve their own ends. Capitalists know how to capitalize—on everything, of course, but especially human beings. Nothing could be more to their advantage than getting the oppressed to identify with their oppressors. But the middle class is catching on to the scam, and their anger is growing.

Once, at the absolute bottom of my life, which cratered aptly during Reagan's reign, I was reduced to working for the Internal Revenue Service (It was the only job I could get, because the government didn't care if I was grossly overqualified—more for less, in their view—and hired me on the basis of my test scores), and the sad schlump who was my "team leader" told a group of us new drudges to "make the IRS's goals" our goals.

Fat chance, I thought, since the IRS sucks blood from the average citizen for transfusion to huge corporations that claim to be anemic or to businesses that, because of uncreative accountants, make the mistake of actually paying some taxes now and then but get refunds by taking advantage of sweetheart tax laws (the fat cats never got bothered in the Eighties, because it was understood that the poor must support the rich; anything otherwise was unthinkable heresy). We were urged to become myrmidons of the mammoth and generally despised (with good reason) governmental agency, the powerful arm of an unfeeling machine that is controlled and manipulated by the people who own this country and run it for their advantage.

And so day after dismal day, until I was able to escape, I sat among scores of other hapless drones in front of a computer terminal whose screen was ruining my eyes and giving off radiation capable of doing who knows what to internal organs. So people get cancer and leukemia, so what? Thousands more are ready to take their places and keep the machines running day and night. To say that I hated this job would be gilding the lily, and I looked for ways to sabotage the system. Bite the hand that feeds me? I wanted to chew it off. Because of rigid controls and defensive computer programming, I couldn't do much, but I did what I could, and I like to imagine some devoted nerd is still working to straighten out the kinks I left behind.

But most of the people there, even though they disliked their jobs and despised the place, were victims of the Protestant Work Ethic and too scared to be anything but conformists and docile employees always ready to say "yes" to any order. They were so conditioned to do as they were told that I began to think of IRS as a prison—and in many ways the image is fitting: the grounds are patrolled around the clock and the building is controlled by armed guards who will not let anyone enter or leave without an appropriate badge of servitude, and the inmates are regimented into lockstep behavior that thwarts individuality the way water thwarts fire. In any event, the career people, whom I viewed as "lifers," had for the most part found a way to move zombie-like through their shifts and, I suppose, to make the best of a bad deal the way a hopeless convict does by sacrificing desire to necessity. After all, no one has ever aspired to be an IRS employee; just imagine a youngster saying, "When I grow up I want to be a tax examiner for the IRS." The very idea chills the blood.

About those badges, IRS employees were required to wear them at all times during their shifts, and some workers grew so accustomed to them—like becoming accustomed to a wart—that they wore them thoughtlessly into stores and other public places after work, but most took them off and stuffed them out of sight upon exiting the prison, ashamed to be seen in polite company with such emblems of slavery. Once I observed a fellow at the post office with his badge prominently displayed, a man who had obviously given up, and when someone asked how he liked working at the IRS, which I thought was like asking how one might like herpes, he responded equivocally: "The benefits are good." Only a fool could say "I love the job—it's exciting and fulfilling." No, he couldn't possibly *like* the job, so he had to find some justification for doing it, and he looked to the "benefits," *i.e.*, retirement plan, vacation and sick leave allowance, medical coverage—he'll need a good hospitalization policy because the job is guaranteed to make him sick. So he sells his soul for the "benefits," and modern slavery is defined by this less than Faustian exchange.

"The highest reward for work," according to John Ruskin, "is not what you get for it, but what you become by it." Doubtless, the young man, reconciled to his lot and embracing his "benefits," was no philosopher, but he understood and accepted American pragmatism; John Ruskin was of no consequence, and more's the pity.

About badges in general, I see now that many salespeople and supermarket checkers are forced to wear nameplates by a management that figures such a ploy will make their business seem, if not more personal, at least more human. But badges and nameplates are sure signs of alienation and are in truth dehumanizing, but the bosses are so blinded by profit that they cannot perceive the damage they do to humanity. Pets and cattle wear tags or are branded; human beings deserve better treatment—but they will never get it as long as they lower their necks for the master's yoke.

Getting back to Epstein's essay that sings the praises of giving effort, the father also said, "If you don't like your work, you're in trouble." Those words are achingly true, and Epstein, who has been more fortunate than most in his occupations, acknowledges this truth but fails to recognize that millions of working people are in trouble, stuck in unpleasant, ungratifying, and undesirable jobs that are very much like quicksand. He makes a point of attacking—gratuitously it seems to me—Studs Terkel's authentic book, *Working*, calling it "tricked-up" and doubting, without offering any evidence to support his skepticism, that the book presents a picture that is "anywhere near accurate." Epstein refuses to believe what is right before his eyes because, admittedly, he likes his own work and is contented; therefore, he assumes that most people regard their work in a similar fashion. Obviously, he is very comfortable in the offices of *The American Scholar*—not much soul-killing suffering in the editing and writing of essays—but I'd like to see him forced into some of the grueling and humiliating jobs that Terkel brings to our attention by interviewing the human beings who do them over and over until they die, often before their time, their bodies exhausted and broken, their spirits defeated. It's hard to put a happy face on a worn out and ruined life.

Like so many other comfortable intellectuals, Epstein, who knew early on that he "would not work at a labor job permanently," and was merely "a visitor there, a tourist on the payroll," simply does not comprehend or make any attempt to understand what happens to people who are not "visitors" and "tourists" like himself, but virtual slaves to menial jobs that offer no hope but survival. He believes—or wants his readers to believe—that dignity and happiness can be found in the most degrading drudgery, and he cites the fictional experience of Ivan Denisovich, the Russian prisoner who is a model of human fortitude in Solzhenitsyn's tribute to the human spirit, who works "under the worst possible conditions of cold, hunger, and fear," and who triumphs over his imposed slavery with "hugely impressive dignity." Although unintentional, a comparison between the gulag where the protagonist is imprisoned (which aims to turn him into a "jackel") and the marketplace for employment is strikingly fitting, because the greatest achievement in both is to remain human in an inhuman setting where the individual's fundamental decency is tested. When one has to invoke slavery and imprisonment to bolster an argument for personal sacrifice, the argument is misleading. Apparently Epstein would like Ivan to be a model for the poor workers in this country, but he shows no more understanding of Solzhenitsyn's novel than he shows of Arthur Miller's *Death of a Salesman*, which he potshots as "lumpy and mawkishish," saying he wishes Miller could have met his work-loving father before writing about Willy Loman. The implication is that Miller would have been "enlightened" and a great American play would have been aborted. Egad.

If fiction and drama can be invoked to make a point, I have a veritable arsenal of literature at hand to demolish the idea of work as a rewarding end in itself. With no effort, I can immediately fortify my argument with Zola's *Germinal*, Melville's "Bartleby, the Scrivener," any number of Charles Dickens novels, Upton Sinclair's *The Jungle*, Steinbeck's *Grapes of Wrath*, and a battery of contemporary novels from Robert Ward's *Red Baker* to John Sayles' *Union Dues*. But I suppose the privileged Mr. Epstein would find these works "tricked-up" and "nowhere near accurate." What he knows of accuracy wouldn't fill a flea's ear, yet he smugly expatiates on the topic of work for an audience that has acquired most of its knowledge of the subject from other printed sources, from words rather than work. *The American Scholar*, after all, is read by the soft and secure, those whose experience of labor is even more limited than Epstein's and whose knowledge in general is more theoretical than practical, people whose experience is with language, not labor.

Bruce Jackson's novel, *The Programmer*, provides a vicarious pleasure for the reader in its high-spirited depiction of one man's successful use of a computer—the very emblem and device of control—against the giant conglomerates for personal gain and redistribution of wealth. Scores of fictional characters, major and minor, share a desire to use whatever inadequate sword they have against the corporate dragon whether or not they ever muster the courage to act. *Not a Through Street* presents a "guy who worked for the phone company," another disaffected worker who "was a quiet subversive. He wanted to sabotage the system, and his enemy was his employer." Evidently, corporations are breeding widespread resentment within and without as golden chains are recognized to be chains all the same (for a series of real-life "Anecdotes of Dissatisfaction, Mischief and Revenge," see the book, *Sabotage in the American Workplace*).

Shoplifting, a subversive act, has become epidemic, and retail businesses claim the incidence of theft is increasing at an alarming rate. From coast to coast, irate consumers are fighting back by ripping off the companies that they feel have been ripping them off for years. This behavior indicates not so much a decline in morality as it does a perception of business as uncaring and unbridled *taker*. Frustrated and angry, consumers are conducting a guerrilla war because they are tired of giving, of being gouged and cheated, and because they feel helpless to fight back any other way. They see the callous and uncaring way companies operate and try to reciprocate, giving them a taste of their own rotten medicine—and their behavior indicates that the employers still control morality, only now it is their *example* that is followed.

The best way to remedy our national problem is for the massas to set a different example. (In a recent book, *The Overworked American*, Harvard economist Juliet Schor examines the way business and culture promote workaholism; she also shows what can be done to regain our share of free time.) The BIG ought to change, to become more human, or at least more humane. "A great business is really too big to be human," commented Henry Ford, but it is going to have to become humane to survive, much less prosper. We are all in this mess together, but the BIG leaders share the greatest responsibility, and they are going to have to do something constructive and decent, or else. We have witnessed the collapse of communism in the soviet union, a crumbling that resulted from widespread dissent and a pervasive conviction that the system was not working and needed to be dismantled. Many American journals, in an orgy of self-congratulatory preening, oblivious to any lesson that might be gained, rejoiced at the failure and praised our own system as if unaware of its steady decline—"slump" is the euphemism most often applied—and heedless of the deep fissures in its foundation and the increasing signs of dissatisfaction and dysfunction all around them: unchecked inflation, more than eight million workers unemployed, crime spreading in all directions, waning faith, a sluggish economy, leaders with no solutions, and an ever growing body of angry workers, many of whom are subversive—not to mention a national debt of over 5 trillion dollars that is an unnatural cancer on the future. The apologists for the system, such as Epstein, are no longer convincing, and cannot hold at bay the rising tide of discontent on our own shores.

I have used Epstein's essay as an example of the blindness with which intelligent people serve the ends of a system that is corrupt and destructive. These people are drummers who do not see the sore and aching feet of the marchers and do not want to see the rocky road that millions are trudging on with little or no hope for anything more than a hardscrabble existence. To be sure, editors and journals all across the country periodically extol the joys of work and the greatness of capitalism, but they are sounding hollow to people who are through giving, who feel swindled and don't want to be lied to and tricked anymore. The number of malcontents is growing, and the disgruntled and disillusioned are going to be a force that cannot be disregarded by the BIG. The American dream no longer holds us in thrall (when realized, as so many novelists have told us, it is false and empty, a sham; but for most Americans, the dream never came true). Still, we want to believe in the dream, and our desire—our *need*—to believe in it is the weakness that the massas have exploited for so long. It's the unreliable carrot at the end of the stick that has kept the horse of labor slogging along.

In "The River," a poignant song about working people and the circumstances that keep the poor, Bruce Springsteen asks, "Is a dream a lie if it don't come true, or is it something worse?"

It's something worse.

The Coming Revolution   Mac Lojowsky

Today I installed a four thousand dollar
cherry-paneled refrigerator,
then fine-sanded the new,
five thousand dollar black walnut mantle,
and was careful not to dirty
the fresh, six thousand dollar
marble countertop.

This all went on inside
a brick condominium that cost more
than a half million dollars.
It was locked behind a tall,
wrought iron fence,
among other brick condominiums
on the city's west side.

The man who owned the place
was a silk-handed millionaire
who has never worked a day
in his inherited life.

His wife drank scotch,
wore big diamond earrings,
and supervised my work
from a zebra-skinned chair.

At quitting time, the husband and wife
had been gone golfing two hours.
I stole away upstairs
to their new, still in the plastic,
top-of-the-line king-sized mattress,
and cut open the plastic wrapping.

I visualized the fall
of a economic system that thrives
on four thousand dollar refrigerators
and gated communities of millionaires.
I visualized smashing marble countertops,
tearing down wrought iron fences.

© Photo by Fred Lonidier

Part Two

Brothers: Grief and Happiness

Sorrow Knows this Dress

Minton Sparks

Sorrow knows this dress,
cotton-made, time-torn.
It's not the color or the cut that cries out
but the slack-shouldered emptiness, a scarecrow
exposed to a parched dusty yard.
Reveals more than a house-dress should.
Around the hemline, shame shows.
Embarrassed, a shy collarbone
protrudes. Pale daisy-print cloth
forgetful now of summer days,
blowing on the line between the sweet gums.
Breasts nag at the waistline—
hungry old mares.
Belly slack from child bearing and buttered bread.
The knees poke through,
cotton worn so thin it shines.
I wrestle this place
—this cotton-field-of-a-dress.

Mississippi Moonshine   **Minton Sparks**

"She'd a been the first issued
a DUI on the Mississippi"
My gypsy used to say.

Out on the bow of
a muddy Mississippi barge
on a sweltering Delta night
Thelma ached for anchor.
Nipping hidden moonshine
beneath a cloud of weary.

Been cooking in the kitchen since sun-up,
ankles swollen beyond worn banks of her shoes.
The dark drank the color
from her yellow hair, as it fell
oily in whiskey curls around a
once beautiful face.

Thelma was cursed by extremes:
beauty, penchant for strong anything,
and barge kitchen men.

Drunk, driving right down the middle
of the muddy waters,
she begged the sky a favor.
The answer came on moonshine fumes
written against the night,

"Being too much of yourself, needs no forgiveness."

My Parents: Snoring

I

A hailstorm leaves
dents in the trees,

and still
they sleep.

Bent and pushed
to the ground,

some branches brush
the grass, a sound

like her throaty alto,
lyrics to the beat

of branches
against the windows,

a humble cry
for escape

like his nasal bass.
I know this tune

by heart,
have never known them

apart
from exhaustion.

Nelson Demery, III

II

Tiptoe like
a drizzle trailing

a sudden
storm. Whisper

with the winds
a new song

of callused hands
at rest:

may their sleep be
a peaceful slumber,

may they never dream
of scrubbing.

Felon   **Wanda Coleman**

my heart comes thru my skin

they've snatched my kids

if the police catch me home i'm sunk
(when handcuffed the first and greatest itch
is my nose)
better find some place to spend the night
the car
sleep behind the wheel behind the
apartment building in winter night cold
doors locked
i wake but the scream goes on

can't tell mama about this

crimester. only crime i'm guilty of trying to
play alice straight in crookedland

money bitch. can't get hold of it

if the cops stop me it's jail without bail
drive. careful. one eye on the road
one eye on the rear view. one eye on tomorrow

help county hospital psycho ward
the gay psychiatrist tells me "write a book"
my employer saves my neck cuz it's his wallet
his attorney thinks i'm a cut above scum
the foster mother smiles beneath her black bouffant wig
and tells me my children are well behaved

court the judge is black-robed and pleasant
nods. extenuating circumstance (so rare to see
a nigger here on somethin' other than homicide dope
prostitution rape robbery)
yes
the records are sealed

they almost took me out this time

provide he said. provide
the condition of my release/getting them back
in my custody

i must provide (try to make a dollar outta 15¢)

i will. with difficulty
but i will

Dry Creek Runs Wet in Winter   Sandra Lee Stillwell

To stand
at her husband's kitchen sink,
beside the hot plate
scrubbing vegetables they will eat,
she is transformed
as Dry Creek runs wet in winter.

To stand
at her husband's kitchen sink,
crafted of white porcelain,
scrubbing the vegetables he grows
for food and money,
she looks out the window,
and feels like she is sailing a small boat,
bucking the current
as Dry Creek runs wet in winter.

To stand
at her husband's kitchen sink,
crafted of white porcelain,
scrubbing the vegetables he grows,
the swollen creek raging toward the window,
she becomes dizzy, nauseous,
and is forced to move away from that view,
as Dry Creek runs wet in winter.

To stand
at her husband's kitchen sink,
crafted of white porcelain,
scrubbing the vegetables he grows,
she can feel the salmon fight the current
back to their place of birth,
to spawn
and she wonders what it would feel like
to go back home
or simply to spawn
as Dry Creek runs wet in winter.

Sick Child   Diana Joseph

She'll remember this as a friendlier time: he's coughing, but only because he can't not cough. His cough is a barking seal; it's a clogged drain. It's her name in the middle of the night. As tempting as it may be to ignore him, to put a pillow over her head, to pull the blankets over her face, to close her eyes and count to ten in every language she knows–English, Japanese, Pig Latin–he'll still cough; she'll still hear him.

He's so rarely sick that she isn't sure what she's supposed to do. In a strange way, this is a good thing: he's rarely sick because of her cautious parenting–a new toothbrush every month, anti-bacterial hand soap, long walks in mountain air, Flintstones vitamins. She's a mother without health insurance. Should she plug in the vaporizer? Fill the bathroom with steam? Rub him down with Vicks?

She was once like him, a child with a winter cold. She was a girl in western Pennsylvania, and her father did all of the above, plus he made her lie face down on the ironing board. He hoisted up the end her feet dangled from, while her mother held her legs down, and her brothers pounded on her back. Near her head was a stainless steel pan for her to spit the phlegm from her lungs into. This remedy worked because her father believed a cold could be bullied. *Mind over body,* he said, thus ensuring no one ever brought home bronchitis again.

Her son is sitting on the edge of his bed, a thin sheet draped around his shoulders. He's wearing only his underwear. His face is pale, his eyes are glassy. His hair is slicked back with sweat. "Where are your pajamas?" she asks.

"I got hot."

Does he have a fever?

Touching his forehead, she can't tell. She imagines the long search for the thermometer, sticking it under his tongue, his protests, the lights she'd have to turn on. "Just relax," she tells him. "Take it easy. You'll be all right, I promise." She carries him back to her bed, where she strokes his damp hair, murmuring to him, and they both fall asleep only to both wake minutes later.

He's coughing.

It's a terrible sound.

There's a bottle of children's cough syrup in the medicine cabinet, but she knows it's expired. She hasn't given him any since that night more than a year ago, the night when his father, who was then her husband, went to a funeral back in Pennsylvania, some old maid aunt dead by natural causes. This was the night her lover was coming over, and she wanted her son to go to bed early and sleep soundly. She thought mixing a spoonful of cherry-flavored cough syrup in his Pepsi would help him along. It was a trick she'd picked up from a talk show, a white trash mother accused of doing it so she could go party, and the audience hissed and booed.

But the trick backfired. Instead of making him groggy, instead of knocking him out, the cough syrup made him hyper. *Supercharged*, his grandmother would have said. *Wired for sound.* It was after midnight before she finally got him to sleep, and when her lover did come over, she was so tense and agitated, feeling so guilty–*I slipped my own kid a Mickey!*– that she just wanted to get the whole thing over with so the night could end.

Her son is still coughing; she still hears him.

When will this end?

Her son is six years old, and as far as he knows, his cough could be with him always, like the scar on his elbow from the time he fell out of a tree at the park, like his mother's boyfriend, like the note Mrs. Quintera sent home saying he's a glue-eater, like the scar near the corner of his left eye from the time he doesn't know what happened. His cough could stay inside him and grow with him, getting bigger as he does. It could follow him around like the puppy he's always wanted but can't have because they live in an apartment complex, or like the maybe-someday baby brother or sister his mother occasionally pines for which is something he doesn't ever want. His cough could be his friend, his ally, his trusted servant. He coughs, and his mother listens.

His eyelids flutter and close, and when he pushes them open, he's not in his bed or his mother's. She's moved him again: now he's lying under a blanket on the couch, and the television is on, blue light in a dark night room, and his mother is stretched out on the floor beneath him, smoking a cigarette and staring at the ceiling. He disapproves of her smoking and coughs a little to let her know. If his mother didn't smoke, they could buy a house and a washing machine of their own. He could have a dog. But the little cough turns into a big one: it sucks all the air out of him, filling his lungs with barbed wire and brittle twigs and dusty cotton and flecks of tobacco from the bottom of his mother's purse. *You wanted to scare her*, his cough tells him. *It's your own fault.*

His mother sits up and takes his hand. She's counting in the Japanese he learned in karate class and then taught to her: *ichi, ni, san, shi, go.* But that was before his parents got divorced. "Just relax," she tells him. "Remember: mind over body."

On the day of the scar near his eye, during the ride to the hospital, his mother counted to three hundred and eighty-eight. One minute, he was at her boyfriend's house, where they'd gone to do laundry, and he was all by himself in the back yard, sent there by her boyfriend and told to play quietly.

The next minute, he was in the emergency room, where a doctor with a needle that looked like a fishing hook was stitching up a small but deep hole near the corner of his left eye. *Can you tell me what happened?* the doctor said. He told her he didn't know. The doctor asked his mother to step out of the room. *Now will you tell me what happened?* the doctor said, and he told her, *Something did, but I don't know what.*

His father called from Pennsylvania, and his grandfather called, and there was also Mrs.Quintera, and the check-out girl at the grocery store, and the old lady at the bank, all asking, *What happened?* All saying, *C'mon, you can tell me.* His grandfather told him that if he didn't 'fess up, then Santa Claus wouldn't come to Colorado, nor the Easter Bunny, nor the Tooth Fairy, and his mother, who'd been listening on the other extension, said, *Bullshit*, and told him to say good-bye to Grandpa. His mother's boyfriend said, *That kid knows good and well what happened; he just won't tell.* His father said, *Where was Mom?*

Right now, his father is asleep in a bed fifteen hundred miles away; his father doesn't even know that the best boy in the world can't stop coughing. Outside, a car glides across the icy parking lot. Inside, light from the television flickers, and his mother is counting. "Ichi, ni, san, shi, go," she says. "Go! Go away, you stupid cough. Get out of Carleton's body."

She sounds mad. She doesn't know his cough is something he can see when he closes his eyes. His cough looks like a thistle stuck to a sock, a burr stuck to a shoelace. It's holding a long pointy stick like a spear; it's twirling the spear like a baton. The spear is tied to a weeping willow branch with a shoelace, and his cough flicks it at him like a whip, narrowly missing his eye. His cough is saying, *Ichi, ni, san, shi, are you sure you want me to go? If you let me stay, I'll be your best friend.*

"Mom?"

"Just close your eyes. Breathe, sweetheart. I want you to relax."

His mother's voice is low and smooth. Her hands are soft. Her eyes are brown, like his.

She's counting, and he's listening. He's relaxing, like she wants. She's turning up the heat; the furnace clanks and moans. Hot dry air kicks out. His breathing turns slow and shallow.

He's asleep.

But for how long?

His mother is sitting on the drafty floor, watching him. Her son is sleeping, but not peacefully. He's wheezing. He's grinding his teeth. His eyelids are fluttering, his eyeballs are rolling; he's the witness to something happening in a dream. The scar near the corner of his eye is pink, but the doctor told her it'll eventually fade, and as he grows, and his skin stretches, it will slide across his face. *My guess is he gouged himself with a sharp object*, the doctor said. His scar is a small dent, no bigger than a pencil eraser, and she runs her finger over it.

He's the only child she's ever been around, so she doesn't have any basis for comparison, but he strikes her as a strange little kid, so dreamy and unfocused, like the day she ran her fingers through his hair and found it was stiff, as if he hadn't rinsed the shampoo out of it, and when she asked him, he said, *I must've forgot.* Or like the night she went in to check on him before going to bed, and there he was, uncovered, asleep, and stripped of his pajamas, with a brown teddy bear stuffed down the front of his under-wear. Or like the day his teacher sent home a note saying that he'd first squirted glue on Joe's arm, was warned, and then was caught, "gleefully lapping a substantial amount of glue out of his cupped palm."

Your son is a glue-eater, said her lover in a way that, to her, seemed critical and unfriendly. She'd replied, *Maybe so. But every class needs one*, and she kept the note, smoothed out the creases and put it in her son's baby book, along with the strands from his first haircut and the hospital discharge papers from the day he got his stitches. That day had been almost a month ago, and still, her son's father won't let it go, saying, *Don't think I'm paying for this. Where were you? He could have lost an eye. You don't even know what happened. Why weren't you watching him?*

"I was in the basement," she tells her sleeping son. "You got hurt during the rinse cycle, and I was adding fabric softener. Or maybe it hap-pened when I was sitting on the couch, kissing and being kissed." She runs her finger across her son's brow, then kisses his scar. "I don't remember," she says.

Her lover is in his fifties; he's never been married, and he is not a lover of children. In a strange way, this is a good thing: it protects her from her whims, from the stirring she feels when confronted with the babies she sees in department stores and on television and in her own mind. Her lover pays for her birth control, reminding her that it's important to take her pill at the same time every day, thus ensuring there are no accidents. *Happy or otherwise*, he says. *I don't want anyone else. I only want you*, and this, too, is good. It protects her from the jealousy she felt last June, when her son and his father were together, and her son seemed to forget about her, hugging his father at the Pittsburgh Greyhound station, not returning her wink, not holding her hand, his father needing to remind him, *Say good-bye to Mom. Tell her you'll see her in three months*, before she boarded her bus back to Denver. It's the same jealousy she'd felt only moments after her son was born, and her husband left her lying there on the table, alone, sweaty and exhausted; he stood with his back to her, cradling the baby in his arms. By July, she missed her son terribly, much more than she'd antici-pated, and her lover said, *It's really good with just you and me.*

I can't be with that kid every second of the day, she'd told his father. *He's fine. He didn't lose his eye. Isn't that what's important? Does it really matter how it happened?*

Her son's father said, *You tell me.*

Outside, snow is still falling. She gets up and looks out the window to where her neighbors, a college girl and her boyfriend, are drunkenly coasting across the icy parking lot on plastic lunch trays, the boyfriend giving the girl a hard push, the girl on the tray, sliding, spinning to a stop.

Inside, the apartment is unbearably hot; the living room is shrinking. It's the dry heat, the noise from the television. It's the flickering light, the blankets heaped on the floor, her sock wet from the glass of water she tripped over. Her face feels greasy; her mouth tastes sticky; she needs to brush her teeth. It's her son, who is awake, filling the room with his croupy cough.

Why is he sick?

Her son doesn't know. His cough says, *You know good and well*, and the spear attached to the whip flicks at him like the forked tongue of an angry snake.

"Mom?" he says.

His mother doesn't say anything. She's pulling the curtain back over the window; she's changing the channel on the television. She hits the mute button. His mother is yawning, propping another pillow behind his head, then she's turning on the fan over the stove and lighting another cigarette. She sucks smokes in and blows it out. Smoke comes out of her nose and floats around her face.

He misses his dad.

They are two guys who can do whatever they want, like eat popcorn for supper, throw popcorn at each other, and rent movies rated P.G., like the one about the ninja warrior who had a powerful and deadly spear. *You probably won't want to tell Mom about that one*, his father said. They can go to bed wearing sweatpants instead of pajamas, and then wear those same sweatpants the next day, and not just around the house. They can wear them in public, which is something his mother won't let him do because her boyfriend thinks it's white trashy. She called him every day over the summer, her voice tiny and far away, and she told him how much she missed him, how she couldn't wait until he was home with her again, *I don't know what to do without you,* she said, but right now, she's back at the window, staring outside at something he can't see.

"Mo-om!" he says.

He coughs, and it feels like the claws of a thousand alley cats scratching against his throat. *Meow,* says his cough. *You can't have a cat because your mother is allergic to them.* But his grandparents have one, and he petted it over the summer, while his dad sat at the kitchen table talking to them about his mother; they asked him if his mother and her boyfriend ever sent him to his room, or outside, or if they ever turned on cartoons for him to watch so they could take a nap together. *Is her boy-friend mean to you? Is her boyfriend mean to her? Does he ever spend the night? How often does he come over?*

I don't know, he told them. *I can't remember.*

"Mom?" he says.

She doesn't answer.

Ichi, ni, san, she's forgotten about you, his cough says.

You can always come live with me, his father said. *Say the word, and I'll come get you. Think of the fun we'd have.*

His cough says, *Would you really leave your mother? What would she do without you?* His cough makes him gasp for air. His face is turning red. He's coughing from deep in his lungs; he's hacking, like his lungs are crumbling, and he can't catch his breath. He can't control this or stop it from happening. His body twists, then he's falling off the couch, then his mother snatches him up, and as if by accident, they're outside in the parking lot. He's wearing Spider Man underwear; his mother is wearing a long tee-shirt, and snow flakes melt in their hair.

"Nice night," says a guy with ski goggles around his neck and a bottle of beer in his hand.

"Are you okay?" says a girl sitting on a plastic lunch tray.

"He's sick," his mother says, and she's out of breath herself. "He can't stop coughing."

But he's not coughing.

For now.

How will this end?

His mother thinks it's bound to end badly. Her son is in no shape to go to school in the morning, which means she won't be able to go to work, and her boss, a childless woman, won't be happy with her. He'll sleep most of the day, and by the day after tomorrow, he'll be feeling a bit better, but still not well enough to go to school.

That day won't be a friendly one.

On that day, he'll cough, not because he can't help it, but because she'll be ignoring him. She'll want him to get well, not because he's her son, and she loves him, which is true enough, but because she'll be sick of his sickness. She'll be sick of holding his hand and talking to him in a low smooth voice. She'll get sick of reading him books and watching his videos, of bringing him bowls of chicken noodle soup and glasses of ginger ale. She can already see limp noodles spilled and drying on the kitchen floor, dishes piling up, beds unmade, milk passing its expiration date. She can already hear her mother's voice on the telephone, *Well, dear, if you hadn't de-cided to remain clear across the country*; and her father's, *Make him get up and walk around. Tell him to shake it off. You baby that kid*; and her lover's, *Is he still contagious?*; and her ex-husband's, *How'd he even get sick?* She can already feel the itch in her throat and the ache in her lungs.

Outside, clouds drift across the moon.

Inside, she says, "Carleton, I can make you a cup of tea. That might help you feel better. Would you like that?"

He nods.

Once, mother and son were at the bank, in line at the drive-through window. He was sitting behind her, strapped in a car seat, when he burped, loud and wet, then he puked up pancakes and apple juice. He wasn't quite two years old that day, and he didn't seem sick–just surprised.

She quickly ran through her options: should she hurry up and rush him home, or could she go ahead and make her deposit? There was the rising stink of maple syrup, the beige streaks on his cheeks, and there was also the likelihood of checks bouncing if she didn't immediately get the money in her account.

A car pulled up behind them, and her decision was made.

She spoke to him in a low smooth voice–the same voice her mother had used on her father during the layoffs at Rockwell, the one she'd used on her son's father, who was then only her boyfriend, when she told him she'd missed her period. *It's okay. Everything will be all right.*

He emitted another damp belch, then he turned his face from her. He hiccupped, he was frowning, he was trembling. She knew he wanted to cry, and if he did, it would be explosive, loud and wet. It would fill the car.

Relax, baby, she said. *You'll be okay, I promise.*

He wouldn't look at her. Instead, he looked out the window. As she soothed him, he continued to stare sadly out the window, and in his profile–his forehead wrinkled, his brow furrowed, his bottom lip quivering– she could see what he'd become, how he'd be when he was a man with troubles beyond his control.

Tis Morning Makes Mother a Killer   **Wanda Coleman**

mean

the day grinds its way slowly into her back/a bad
mattress stiffens her jaw

it is the mindless banalities that pass as conversation
between co-workers

her paycheck spread too thin across the bread of
weeks; too much gristle and bone and not enough

blood

meatless meals of beans and corn bread/nightsin the electronic arms of
the tube

mean as a bear

carrying groceries home in the rain in shoes
twice resoled and feverish with flu

it is the early dawn

mocking her unfinished efforts; unpaid bills,
unanswered letters, unironed clothes

tracks
of pain in her face left by time; the fickle high of it
facing the mirror of black flesh

mean as mean can

pushed to the floor but max is not max enough
no power/out of control/anxiety

it is the sun illuminating cobwebs

that strips her of her haunted beauty; reveals
the hag at her desperate hour

children beware

Nora's Needs   **Suzanne Nielsen**

Nora Nephling believed she was born two years and seven months old, which was how old she was when she went to live with her grandma permanently. They lived on Earl Street in East St. Paul, and she called her grandma "Ma." She had a dad that sometimes showed up at their back door, drunk. Nora was my next door neighbor, a year my senior, but from twelve years old and on, she looked old enough to be my own mother.

At nine, Nora already had boobs that poofed out the front of her tight-fitting sweaters and she wore the same color eyeliner, only thicker, as Mrs. Fisher, my second grade teacher. She had another poof on the top of her head from ratting her hair that always frightened me. It looked as though spiders nested in there and they very well may have.

I knew that the Nephling house had bugs because the one and only time I slept over at Nora's, we stabbed centipedes in her basement with a wire hanger that we undid and used like a whip. When Nora pierced the bugs in the center of their bodies, they would arch their backs while moving their legs in a million directions until finally they gave in to death. It seemed like it took forever, watching them die like that, speared on the end of a wire hanger, while Nora said to them, "how do you like that?" Stab, stab. "You think you're so smart, hiding in here like that, if I ever catch you sneaking upstairs, you'll be sorry, you worthless good-for-nothing pieces of shit." Nora carried on like that with a vengeance, while the centipede wiggled to be free until death made it still. Then she would shake the corpse into the toilet and flush it away. I asked her if she thought those centipedes might get even by coming back hundredfold and attacking us for our wrong doings, but she didn't seem too concerned; "Just let the little fuckers come back," she'd said. "Next time I'll spray them with ma's hair spray and their death will linger on."

Nora was the first person I ever heard use the word fuck. I re-member liking how the sound forged itself through her lips and one wet day I came in from outside and told my mama to look at all the fucking worms on the driveway and she slapped me across the face. She told me if I ever used that word again, she'd hit me so hard, I'd forget if I was coming or going. I learned early-on that the things Nora taught me were not things I would then try to teach my own mama.

"That Nora Nephling is a bad influence, a nasty little girl," she said. "She's so bad that even her own mother ran away from her." Until then, I had imagined that Nora's real mama was killed in a car accident, or maybe a motorcycle accident. My mama said that Nora's dad was *good-for-nothing* and that old Mrs.Nephling was just a *good-for-nothing drunk*. I'd never seen old Mrs. Nephling with a bottle of beer but mama told me the coffee mug that Mrs. Nephling always carried with her was her way of hiding the bottle. "That mug's never had a drop of coffee in it," said mama. "It's full to the brim with whiskey." One day I snuck a taste, a day that I snuck over to Nora's without my mama knowing and woowee, that was some strong brew in that mug! That's when I believed mama could be right about the Nephlings. They hid the idea of whiskey. They had a bunch of broken down cars in their driveway, along with broken windows replaced by plyboard. Glitters of broken glass glowed like diamonds in the sunlight on their front steps. They were what mama called *white trash.*

I should have been glad mama steered me away from Nora because I never would have been able to be a school police patrol if I'd hung around her kind. I took my patrol job very seriously. While I was patrolling the corner of Case and Margaret Streets, Nora was standing kitty-corner, smoking cigarettes she'd stolen from her grandma's purse. One time, I turned Nora in to Mr. Zimmerman, the teacher in charge of the school patrol. Mr. Zimmerman was my fifth grade teacher and he liked me fine. All the cool kids had Mr. 'Z,' that's what we called him. The day I turned Nora in for smoking, Mr. Z told me I did the *right thing*. Nora got in all kinds of trouble. Her grandma had to come to school and talk the principal into not suspending her. Old Mrs. Nephling saw me that day in the school hall. I was getting ready to take my patrol flag to the Case and Margaret Street corner. The whites of her eyes offered a warning as she came towards me head-on and said, "So, you like being a tattle-tale. Well, you'll be happy to know Nora's gonna get the whippin' of her life when her father finds out. You'll rot in hell for this, Shell McPhearson." Her lips flapped through her toothless growl and I think she was foaming from the corners of her mouth. I had nightmares for weeks following, always a vision of an extra-large German Shepard, with the head of old Mrs. Nephling running after me, all her teeth in place.

That following Spring, we had what Mama called an April thaw. She sent me out back with a bucket of warm vinegar water, a stack of old, torn diapers and told me to wash the outside windows of our house. Before the screen door slammed, I heard her add, "and don't leave any streaks!"

While I was gagging from the smell of the vinegar water, Nora came outside with a bride gown on. Not a hand-me-down dress-up thing from her grandma's closet, but a new and authentic bride's dress that fit her tight in all the right places. She was hopping on crutches and she had a cast on her left leg that went from under her dress, all the way down to her foot. Her dad was telling her to hurry up, he had errands to run. He yelled at her to stand by the statue of St. Francis in their back yard, next to the broken bird bath so he could take her picture. I could hear her say, "Right here, Daddy? Don't get my cast in the picture, okay?" Sometimes she'd talk baby talk and this was one of those times.

Her dad was a crabby person and he was now yelling for her to shut up. "Go sit on ma's porch then, and hurry up," he told her. I heard the camera click three times, although he may have taken more than three pictures of Nora. "You didn't get my cast in the picture, did you Daddy?" Nora's voice sounded even more baby-like and I never blamed her dad for hitting her over the head that second time she'd asked him the same question. She was stupid, I thought. That's when parents reserved the right to hit you, when you said stupid things over and over again. And when you talked baby talk. It wore thin on their nerves.

I heard Nora's Dad's car engine sound and then he disappeared. Nora hobbled on her crutches over to the chain link fence that separated our properties and bid me hello. I asked her if I could to sign her cast. Mama must of heard me through the open windows because she came outside and said, "Shell, finish that window and get in here. I need you to help me with something." I wanted desperately to find out how Nora broke her leg. I wanted to know why she was dressed like a bride. I wanted to sign her cast. It gleamed bright white in my direction and as I squinted the sun out of the way of my eyes, I noticed that I would have been the first to sign her plastered injury. I didn't dare risk asking her any of those questions. Mama had ears that could hear things I wouldn't even have remembered saying so I hurried to dry the window with a torn diaper and went inside.

What mama had waiting inside for me was her own set of questions. "What did you say to Nora?How come you talked to her after I told you to leave her kind alone?"

Mama had her arms folded in front of her and a tap in her foot. "Those damn Catholics," she said, "it's criminal how they dress up their little girls to be brides of Christ. Who ever heard of anything so ridiculous?"

Brides of Christ?! We weren't church goers, but we had a Bible somewhere in our house. I didn't know how to recite the Hail Mary or take communion, but I knew this much–Christ never married. What was my mama talking about? Whatever was in her mind couldn't stop me from thinking about that dress Nora had on and how I envied her.

Mama handed me a coffee can full of stray buttons. "Find six that look close enough alike," she said. "I need you to sew them on my red sweater." Mama never sewed. She was too impatient and always stuck her skin with the needle. I wanted to tell her to use the spearmint Lifesavers she sucked half-way down and then used to hem the bottom of her black skirt, the one she always wore with her red sweater. I wanted to tell her to replace the Lifesavers with wads of chewed Dentyne gum. She had to have gone through a pack of that a day ever since she tried to lose weight. I wanted to tell her to use the Lifesavers as buttons, at least they'd match. But I didn't tell mama my thoughts. Instead I asked her how Catholic girls got to be Christ's bride. "That sure was a pretty dress Nora was wearing, don't you think, mama?" I asked. "Why don't all girls get bride-of-Christ dresses?"

I remember the look she gave me, a look that said I was too stupid to really be her kid. "Be glad I don't parade you around looking like that," she said snorting air through her nose. "Communion dresses, veils, it's a stupid religion," she ranted, "and that's why Catholic girls grow up so promiscuous." I didn't know what mama meant by promiscuous but I thought it might be related to stupidity. Thank God I wasn't Catholic! I was my dad's child which Mama said was reason enough for me being stupid, but to add on top of that the idea of being Catholic, I'd have been too stupid for my own good. Oh, but to wear one of those scaled-down bride's dresses. I so wanted to feel the dress against my skin. To have a veil cover my thin brown hair. I would have even learned to use crutches if I could have been Nora for just that afternoon, sitting on her grandma's porch surrounded in pretty lace.

Mama said that the church didn't give those dresses away. "You paid a good price for those. Mrs. Nephling would rather spend her money on communion dresses and bingo than fix up that dump they live in," she said. "Like that's going to get them into heaven!" Mama was always sure about who would make it to heaven and who wouldn't and according to her, no Catholics ever would. I hoped I wouldn't grow up and marry someone Catholic. I didn't want to play bingo. I didn't want to live in a dump or drink whiskey from a coffee mug. I didn't want to have really stupid, promiscuous kids. But I did want to feel the lace of that dress, even if it scratched my legs raw, so I knew I would sneak over to the Nephling's sometime and talk Nora into letting me try it on. Sometime when her grandma wasn't home, because her grandma didn't like me any more than my mama liked Nora.

I never did get over to Nora's to try that dress on. Winter came, and I never saw Nora outside. I would see her in school, but she rarely glanced my way. One day after school, Nora's house was surrounded by police cars. I heard a police radio crackling in the otherwise afternoon stillness and spotted three cops in Nora's front yard. "Gunther P. Nephling, come out the front door with your hands above your head," I heard a cop say over a megaphone. Other cops were like frozen toy soldiers surrounding the house, with their guns pointed towards both doors. I knew they were waiting for Nora's Dad, who must have done something really bad. The door flung open. No air hinge gathered it back closed, and Nora's dad took the two cement front steps in his battered Harley Davidson boots both at the same time. He had his arms stretched over his head, turned around to kick the door closed, then headed towards the cops with a lit cigarette dangling from the corner of his mouth. "Here I am, you sonsabitches," he screamed. He must have gotten into his mama's whiskey mug for he was swerving down that sidewalk as carefree as a feather in the wind. The cop that talked into the megaphone reached up and grabbed Mr. Nephling's wrists, pulled them together and snapped on thick metal cuffs. Two cops led him into a squad car. I remember his hands, latched together behind him, folded as though he was praying to his Catholic God. One of the cops pushed Mr. Nephling's head down like he was a jack-in-the-box and gave him a quick shove into the car. "Hey, man, easy," I heard him say to the cop. The car door closed and the radio was screeching.

Mama opened the front door, motioned for me to get in the house, and reluctantly I did. "Those good-for-nothing Nephling's," she said, "Now they got the whole St. Paul Police Force over there. And you're out there, gawking at the lot of them! I'm telling you, Shell, from now on, if I catch you even so much as looking in their direction, I'll make it so you'll wish you hadn't." Then mama went about her cleaning, singing with Kate Smith that was playing on the Hi-Fi. I went into the bathroom, and snuck a peek out the window. From our bathroom window you could see into Nora's Front room. There was Nora, curled up like a cat in the torn, black vinyl recliner. She was chewing at her fingernails which made me think of Mr. Nephling's locked up hands. I sat on the floor of the bathroom, hands behind my back, pressed up to the cold, cement wall and applied as much pressure as I could. The pain and self-induced confinement tormented me.

I heard Mama just outside the bathroom door bellow along with Kate's recording of *America the Beautiful*, no doubt holding over her heart that old diaper she used as a dust rag. When the live recorded version of the song was finished, I heard mama say to her imaginary crowd, "Thank you, and God Bless. The bathroom door opened so fast, I was almost sucked up off the floor. Nora's silhouette was broken from my view when the window shade was pulled down with a snap of my mama's wrist. Mama slapped my face and screamed, "Don't fuck with me, Shell! You keep your nose out of the Nephling business." It scared me, not so much the slap. She had forewarned me enough that I should have known better. What scared me was how much of Nora's ways had crept into the bodies of us all.

Nora's needs stretched beyond the "No Trespassing" sign taped to her front door. After the day her Dad was hauled away, Nora never took to smiling. Her face grew bitter and her butt grew big. She smoked Camel Straights and drank blackberry brandy in the bathrooms at school. One day at the North door of Hazel Park Jr. High School, Nora was beating the crap out of Cookie Foryes, and Cookie had a reputation for being one tough bitch. She was holding Cookie's face down on the pavement with her foot while slugging Cookie's ribs with her fist. She was saying stuff to Cookie like, "How does that feel, huh bitch? You want to fuck with me, I'll set you straight." Nora looked old to me that day. Her hair was died bright yellow, with dark brown roots two inches long growing from her scalp. She wore grown-up clothes, like halter tops and she had real boobs with a cleavage and all. If she ever caught me looking at her in the halls or by her house, she'd always say, "What you lookin' at, Shell from Hell?"

Nora started to wear makeup even before Jr. High, but by ninth grade, her skin soaked so much of it up that she got a bad case of zits. One day she came to school after having shaved off her eyebrows and drawing black pencil-thin fake ones in place of her real ones. There was a shadow from where the real ones had once been, and when they started to grow back, it reminded me of what I remember my Dad's face looking like after a weekend of fishing up North with his friends and no razor. "You're not sleeping in my bed," Mama would say to Dad. "Get rid of the Daniel Boone look." Mama liked a clean shaven face on a man.

Unlike Mama, Nora wasn't quite so fussy about who crawled into bed with her because by May of ninth grade, her stomach was the size of the Indian mounds at the park. Before school let out for summer vacation, Nora disappeared. I heard through my mama's phone conversations that Nora went to stay with the nuns somewhere and that a nice Catholic family adopted her baby. The thought of having a baby horrified me. I hadn't even started menstruating and Nora had pushed out two arms, two legs and a head from that little opening where the blood eventually comes!

I thought a lot about Nora. I wondered if she would ever come back to Earl Street and sure enough, she did. She returned that Fall with the same scour on her face that her dad carried. I wondered if her dad was still alive and if he knew she had a kid at a nun convent.

Old Mrs. Nephling fixed up the windows and front door of the house and sent Nora to work. How I found out Nora had a job was when I went down to the Earl Street Grocery store and there was Nora, behind the counter smoking a cigarette, working out a crossword puzzle from one of those magazines they sell in the grocery stores. My mama had sent me there to get a can of corn for supper. Nora rang it up, "33 cents," she said. She wouldn't look at me, just took my dollar bill and counted back to me the change. "34, 35, 40, 50, and a dollar. Thanks," she said then went back to her crossword puzzle. I stood there for a minute. There were so many things I wanted to say to Nora. "Did it hurt terrible to have that baby? Where did your daddy go off to? Are you ever coming back to school? Do you still have your bride dress? Do you want to be friends?" I never asked her any of those questions. I just put the change in my pocket and left the can of corn behind.

© Photos by Suzanne Neilsen

Withoutfits   Nelson Demery, III

When we were little
my sister dressed fashionably
in fleece and silks while I wrinkled
my toes in shoes too small.

Noticing my worn shirts and patched pants,
schoolteachers and churchladies matched
me with neglect
and her with my mother's favor.
Too loudly, they'd whisper
How does the woman afford such
nice things
cleaning the Taylors' toilets?
Why won't she sacrifice
the same for the boy?

When we were small
I went through
winters without a jacket,
doubling shirts I was already
too big for, wishing
the Taylors had a son
who grew as fast
as their daughter.

When Cheri's Father Was Crazy   **Victoria Rivas**

Factories were hiring but Cheri's dad
was crazy. The mothers shook sad-eyed heads
over backyard fences. Family men
did not work on the docks loading cargo.

Cheri's dad did, sometimes left for months on
ships, unloaded, loaded again. Then his
father died, left him an upholstery
shop, the house behind it. The mothers smiled.

Now Cheri's dad would not go away. Now,
he had a business at his doorstep.
He did good work in this new life, with tools,
wood, nails, studs, fabrics, leathers, Naugahyde.

But when customers came, he hid in the
bathroom, smoked cigarettes until they left.
Then, there were mornings in the cramped kitchen
with smells of eggs, coffee, toast, four teenage

voices screaming over rock music and
their mom, loudest of all. Cheri's dad sat
at the table, quiet. Amid the din,
he stacked. Cup. Saucer. Cup. Saucer. Sugar

bowl. Cream pitcher. Butter dish. Salt shaker.
Precariously, they sat, balanced in
the chaotic kitchen. And still, he stacked
as his wife screamed *Stop that! Stop that! Stop that!*

Nothing ever fell. Nothing ever broke.
After a few years the upholstery
shop folded. Cheri's dad went back to work
loading cargo on ships, crazy again.

Uneasy Death

Nan Byrne

My mother smoked
four packs a day
putting it in
taking it out
that was the rhythm of her life
one lit, one waiting
by the stove or coffee cup
never elegant
always broke
she smoked for the nicotine
and the Raleigh coupons
when I was a child
I closed my eyes each night
to a picture
my mother at the kitchen table
pretty in jeans
wearing a pin-up turban
hard at work sorting
cigarette packages
from paper slips
cellophane rustling
in her fingers
like dry leaves
People say
a picture is worth
a thousand words
as if
the value of that picture
to me
could ever be found
in words
But if it were
those words
might be these:
who thought it was
a fair trade
a pair of lungs
for a blender
a life

for a pen and pencil set
who thought
it was a good business
to take a mother
from her daughter
to leave only
the weight of ashes
in her hand

Ronald Reagan Cheese   **Allen Frost**

Living dollar to dollar on minimum wage and raising
two daughters, she was entitled to every Friday
at the Food Bank. They gave her two bags of vegetables
and bread and some dented cans of tomato sauce.
It was alright, food wasn't easy to come by.
No matter how poor they were, she didn't want
her daughters to think America was against them.
Like everything else, the price of food had to be
kept high, it had to be competitive—fields
had to go unplanted, silos and dairies had to
let their produce rot. That was how it had to be.
But the president cared enough to pull
a couple thousand pounds of American cheese
from a warehouse in Wisconsin and send it
out on trucks and trains to the small
number of needy out there. The brittle
newspaper clipping stayed taped to their fridge
until the memory of cheese ran out.

Brothers: Grief and Happiness   Thom Tammaro

My brothers—one named for the great Venetian traveler,
and the other for our grandfather who passed through
the Great Hall at Ellis Island with the name "Umberto"
pinned to his chest—work in a chemical plant my oldest
brother tried to organize back in '68 but lost by eight votes.
That means they now work in an open shop; that they have
the right to work, the right to spit blood, the right to have
nose bleeds and wheeze when they cough.

Brothers, do you remember the smell of our father's breath
when he returned home from the night shift at the conveyor
factory, then came to our rooms where we were sleeping, bent
down to kiss us goodnight: smell of flesh, grease, blue J. C. Penny
Big Mac chambray work shirt, Pall Mall smoke, exhaustion?
Was this his blessing bestowed upon us for the life to come?

Brothers, I pray that your lungs gush red; that your bones
rattle clean and white, strong as piano keys; that you cough
hearty and loud into your eighties; that you know the way
it is during my once-a-year visit is the way it always was
for me, and is the way I'll always remember it.
Brothers, I pray that your houses are quiet at night;
that the only sound is the sound of your children's chests
rising and falling in the darkness of their sleep; and that
you always remember to give them the father's blessing:
fleshy, greasy, smoky.

And even if we spit blood and our noses bleed,
if we get only a little happiness from this life,
it's okay because a little grief goes a long way;
but a little happiness stays with us a lifetime.

A Gift of Cookies   Wayne Rapp

On the tops of the hills that nestled together to form the boundaries of the narrow canyons, the wind always blew. In the summer, it was a relief, more of a refreshing breeze that kept the Southern Arizona temperatures from getting out of hand. In winter, though, the wind whipped across the hilltops, bending the juniper bushes and swaying the scrub oak, leaving in its wake a trail of paper trash impaled on the *ocotillo* cactus. On Zacatecas Hill, the dry snow—starved for moisture—would not stick to the ground but would continue swirling through the air, some of it finding its way into the cracks of the old wooden houses, collecting then along the window sills and doorways, even in the corners of the rooms if the gusts were especially strong. Reluctantly, in one quick motion, Beatriz Estrada threw off the blankets that covered her and struggled into a badly-worn robe and slippers. Beatriz shivered and shuffled her short, squatty body off to the hallway where she raised the thermostat from 55 to 65 and silently prayed that the gas would stay on for a while longer.

Jesse Estrada was staring at the ceiling from his hospital bed when she returned. His mouth quivered an inaudible "*buenos días*." It had become difficult for the old lady to look at her husband since his stroke. She saw in his eyes the embarrassment of a man who could no longer feed or clean himself.

"You look better today. Not too cold, I hope. Mr. President says we gotta save the fuel. Let's hope it's not cold like last year, or I'm gonna have to climb in that bed with you to keep us both warm." She laughed light-heartedly.

Jesse raised his right hand in a weak gesture of acknowledgment. He had limited movement there and an equal amount in his right foot. He could chew his food, although somewhat messily, but he had no feeling whatever in his left side.

"I'm gonna get some food for you, then clean you up," she said.

In the kitchen Beatriz busied herself with preparations for breakfast. While water was boiling, she unfolded a wax-paper wrapper and took out two flour *tortillas* and put them on a griddle to warm. Then she poured some whiskey in a cup. She could tell there was little left in the bottle but avoided calculating how little. She dumped a teaspoonful of instant coffee on the liquor, then a dash of powdered milk, before adding the hot water.

As she fed the old man, Beatriz kept up a steady stream of conversation, stopping only to chew her buttered *tortilla* and sip the whiskey-laden coffee. From time to time she tipped the cup to Jesse's lips, wondering if the liquor's glow was warming him. She hoped something cheered him, that something made his day bearable. She looked for a sign on his face but saw only a dribble of liquid emerge from his smacking lips.

"It's hard to believe *la Navidad* comes already," she said. "I didn't even send a Christmas card this year. Everything costs too much." She stopped. It wasn't what she wanted to talk about. She had always tried to keep her husband involved with the events of her day—no matter how trivial—without involving him in the problems, but now it seemed as if the problems were the events of her day.

While she was washing the few dishes from breakfast, Beatriz looked out her kitchen window and down the hill to the canyon below that ran through the heart of San Pedro. She could see the sun, already on the upper canyon, begin slowly pushing the shadows away, illuminating the wooden houses and dry yards that snaked from the top of the hills that surrounded them to downtown. While she watched the early sun, she heard a familiar tapping at the back door. "Come in," she hollered to her neighbor, Ana Duarte.

"Good morning, Beatriz. Boy, it's almost as cold in here as it is outside. Maybe you should have a coat on instead of a robe."

Beatriz did not turn around but continued to busy herself at the sink. "Ah, you get use to it. What you gonna do about it anyway? Cost too much to keep warm. My fat keeps me warm," she said and laughed, turning to face her neighbor. "What you got there?" she asked, pointing to the mounded plate in Ana's hands.

"These are for you," Ana said with a smile. She pulled back tinfoil to reveal a plate of Mexican cookies: sugar and cinnamon-coated *buñuelos*, pineapple-flavored *sevillanas*, and the spiced-chocolate *bestitos de merengue*. They were arranged around a centerpiece of sweet, chewy prickly-pear-cactus candy.

Beatriz gasped in surprise. She knew how time consuming and expensive they were to make. "Why you wanna do that? You take them to your family."

"I made plenty this year. I was gonna bring Christmas dinner to you, but we're going to my daughter's, so you take the cookies," Ana said. "Now let me help you with Jesse. Here it is Christmas Eve, and I got a ton of work to do before we leave town. Next year my daughter can come here."

The Christmas holidays had arrived without Beatriz realizing it. She had lost track of the days, and now it was Christmas Eve. She wondered why she had not heard from her own daughter. She had told Beatriz when they spoke on the phone Thanksgiving that she was sending money for Christmas. "Maybe today," she hoped.

When the women finished bathing and changing Jesse, Ana paused at the back door and asked, "Have you planned your Christmas dinner yet?" Beatriz averted her eyes, and Ana didn't give the old lady a chance to make up an answer. "Well," she continued, "Erica gave me this to give to you for Christmas." She pressed a twenty dollar bill in Beatriz's hand. "She said you'd always been so good to her."

Beatriz's eyes brimmed with tears. "You got a good girl."

"You know, you really should sign up with one of the welfare agencies," Ana said. "There's nothing wrong with getting help when you need it. You and Jesse worked hard all your life."

"Yeah, but I didn't work outta the house, so me and Jesse don't get much Social Security. And he lost his pension when the cement plant closed, so what you gonna do?"

"But there're places. Even the Church."

Beatriz raised her voice. "I don't want charity," she said emphatically. "People gotta tough time takin' care a themselves. Why they gotta support us?"

"You're amazing," Ana said, opening the back door. "*Feliz Navidad* and God bless you."

"And same to you too, and thank Erica." She stared at the money in her hand and smiled. With money still to come from her daughter and a Social Security check due the beginning of January, this twenty dollars could be used for holiday food.

When the phone rang around noon, it startled Beatriz. "Mama. Merry Christmas."

"María!" the old lady answered in an urgent voice. "What's the matter? You never call in the day."

"Nothing's wrong. It's just so hard to get through on Christmas day. How's Papa? Any better?"

"Your *papá* doesn't get better, Beatriz answered, pronouncing the word in the Mexican way. He's as good as he's gonna get."

"How about you?" the daughter asked cheerily. "All ready for Christmas?"

"Yeah, I'm OK. What about those *niños* of yours? *Mis nietos?*"

"Your grandchildren are fine. I told you Mike was in college, didn't I? That's the reason I called. We wanted to send you money this year. Well,..."

The old lady interrupted her. "I don't need your money."

"I didn't say you needed it, Mama. Joe and I planned on it, but we forgot about Mike's tuition for the second quarter. That really threw us for a loop. So,..."

"You keep your money for your family."

"We did get a little package off to you. Hope it gets there in time." She paused. "Mama, when our income tax return gets here, we'll send you some money for sure."

"Don't you worry. Just enjoy *la Navidad* with your family and kiss the kids for me. Now you better hang up or I'll have to send you money to pay your phone bill." The old lady laughed and hung up. When the mail came with a few Christmas cards and a notice—the second one that the gas would be shut off if the bill wasn't paid, Beatriz Estrada knew she must make a decision. The one she had thought about, the one that came to her in the cold, dark mornings when the sun seemed it would never reach the shadowy canyons below, the one she tried to push out of her mind with the incessant Hail Marys, was beginning to make sense.

Tamales were what she needed for her traditional Christmas Eve dinner. Beatriz remembered when Catholics had to fast and abstain from meat on Christmas Eve, and the *tamales* couldn't be eaten until Christmas morning. People came home from Midnight Mass and stood impatiently around the stove waiting for the *tamales* to be steamed. Then they would juggle them in their hands as they peeled the hot corn husks away from the delicious smell of *masa* and wash the *tamales* down with a smile and a cold beer or glass of wine. She remembered how good they tasted for the waiting. Now people ate them for their main Christmas Eve meal instead of fish.

Beatriz dressed, and telling Jesse she had to go to the store, began the long descent from the top of Zacatecas Hill. She moved slowly down the stairs, feeling the cold, hard handrail through her worn mittens. Her knees ached as she transferred weight from leg to leg, trying to be alert to the dangers of the disintegrating concrete. She would not let herself think of the ordeal she would face as she climbed back up the steep steps.

The small Mexican grocery store at the base of the hill carried *tamales* that were homemade by Mrs.Ochoa, the owner's wife. They weren't as good as the ones Beatriz used to make, but that was a long time ago when she could still get around and do the shopping for all the ingredients and stand on her feet cooking the meat and preparing the *masa* and wrapping them in the corn husks to steam. Now what she could find would be good enough. Mr.Ochoa wasn't happy that she wanted only a half dozen; he didn't sell them that way, but finally he relented, muttering something about the holiday spirit.Beatriz rewarded him by buying a small bottle of red wine as well. She left the store with more money in her hand than she had hoped for. Standing on the sidewalk outside, she saw the little Christmas tree. It looked dry and sparse and had a broken branch. A sign read, "Christmas Trees. $5 and up." She stuck her head in the door of the store. "Hey, Francisco.You wanna sell that tree?"

The owner walked to the door. "Which one?"

"The skinny one with the limb broke. You take three dollars for it?"

"It should be worth five dollars, but tomorrow it won't be worth anything. You want it, Mrs. Estrada, take it."

Beatriz pressed the three one dollar bills into the man's hand. "Can you have your boy bring it to my house? I don't got no way to carry it."

The grocer sighed. He needed his son for more important deliveries. He looked at the steps leading up Zacatecas Hill and knew how hard it would be to persuade the boy to carry the tree to the top. Then he looked at Beatriz standing there shivering in her husband's old sweater, her gray hair blowing in the wind but with the biggest smile on her face. "OK. *Feliz Navidad.*"

Once inside the house, with its broken limb tied with green thread, the little tree didn't seem so sparse. With some effort and risk of injury, Beatriz got her decorations down from high in the hall closet. Her string of blue lights had several burned-out bulbs, but on the tree there was sufficient color that the dark bulbs didn't bother her.

Pleased with her progress, she waddled to the bedroom and, seeing that her husband was awake, pushed his hospital bed into the living room. She patted his hand and said, "Looks nice, huh? Bout time we have a real tree."

Beatriz kept up a steady flow of words while she hung the rest of the decorations. It was family sharing for her, a ritual preserved from an earlier, happier time. She let the decorations tug at her memories. She hung the crooked star that María made when she was in the third grade, long before she had gone away to nurses' training, then on to California to have fun and work and have babies, to quit speaking Spanish, and seldom to return to the hardscrabble mining town on the Mexican border that was San Pedro, Arizona.

She held a ceramic elf with BEATRIZ scratched in it to her breast and let the tears flow from her eyes. Jesse Jr. had painted it when he was ten and handed it to her with that big smile of his, eight and a half years before his body was broken in a crumpled car driving home from Mexico on graduation night. She gently moved the elf from her breast to the tree, much as she had moved his cold hand from her wet face and laid it on his still chest twenty years earlier.

She looked at the boy's father. Could he think of his son still? Did his paralyzed body remember planting the seed from which he grew? Jesse's face was distorted awkwardly. He was struggling, but whether with emotion or affliction, she didn't know. Beatriz patted his hand gently and kissed him on the forehead.

In the bottom of the box she spotted the small baby shoes. She grabbed them up and caressed them, and her womb ached for the stillborn baby who never wore them, the one that her mother said looked like her, the one she called Carmelita after her grandmother. How long had it been? She couldn't remember. She only knew that she carried her in her body for nine months and in her heart for the rest of her life—so real now that she felt pressure on her lungs, making it exceedingly hard to breathe. With difficulty, she hung the shoes on the tree and was finished.

She placed their dinner on a TV tray with a candle and fed Jesse in between her own bites. She hoped he could taste the food—especially the *tamales*, since he liked them so well. She didn't bother with the wine during dinner; she had enough trouble trying to feed her husband. When it was obvious that he wanted no more, she took the plates to the kitchen.

Standing over her stove, she looked down at the pilot light, staring past it to its dark source. She exhaled lightly—just a little puff—and watched the blue flame bend away as if beckoning her to follow. With considerable effort, she got down on her knees and opened the oven door. It took her a moment to locate its pilot light, finally running her hand along the oven floor until she felt its warmth. She thought for a moment. How could she put it out? Maybe dump water on it? Leaving the oven door open, she grabbed the top of the stove and pulled herself painfully to an erect position.

She hobbled to the living room with a bottle of wine and two glasses. As she drank, Beatriz kept offering Jesse a sip of wine from his glass. She thought he must like it since very little of it escaped his quivering mouth. She kept talking all the time, unaware really of what she was actually saying, knowing only that it concerned old times, good times. She stopped abruptly when she saw Jesse's eyelids fluttering to stay open, then finally drooping closed.

She stared for a long time at her husband's sleeping face, trying to see there the strong young man who once lived behind those closed eyes, the one who had threatened to fight all her brothers and even her father if they would not let her leave to marry him. She prayed that he would understand that she was the one who had to make the decisions now and whatever one she made would be made for both of them.

Beatriz sipped her wine, leaned back in her chair and closed her eyes. She felt her body begin to relax, and she tried to let her mind become part of it. Drifting. Drifting up, up. Up to softness and safety and serenity. She opened her eyes slightly and saw her little Christmas tree blinking its blue lights at her. She moved her mind to the tree and tried to lose herself in it, letting it wrap its dry little arms around her, holding her and rocking her to sleep. Singing was coming from its branches. Joyful voices. Angels proclaiming that a child was born in Bethlehem. The old lady jerked with a start, suddenly aware of her surroundings. The singing was real; it wasn't coming from the tree but from the canyon below. She limped quickly across the room and opened the front door. Beatriz stood on the porch, the dry snow swirling around her, and watched the candles flickering in a snake-like pattern on the canyon floor. "*Las Posadas*," she said with a smile into the cold night air.

She could picture the scene unfolding below her: children—some of them dressed as angels—leading Chato Figueroa's donkey on whose back sat humbly the lucky young girl chosen to play María, *La Virgen*. Walking beside her, dressed in a long robe and carrying a shepherd's staff, would be the boy husband, José. Behind them followed the people, bundled up, singing carols, and carrying candles to light the way in the dark night. From house to house they would travel, singing their songs and asking for shelter (*posada*). At each house where they are invited to enter, the group would take time to eat and drink what was offered. And so it would go through the evening until the group wound its way to San Antonio Church in time for Midnight Mass.

The *posada* characters asked for the necessities of life: for shelter and for food. That's all Beatriz wanted. Just enough to survive. Just enough for the few more years—maybe only days—that were allotted to her and Jesse.

The old woman went quickly to the kitchen and gently pulled back the foil from the plate of Christmas cookies. She marveled at how good they looked. She smiled at the wonderful smells. Anise and pineapple and cinnamon and all the other sweet-smelling spices. Beatriz turned quickly and closed the oven door, refusing to let her eyes meet the stove's beckoning pilot light. Not this night. She would not think of her difficult life this holy night, only her blessings. And if tomorrow they turned off her gas, then she would burn wood. After all, her mother used to make *tortillas* for a family of twelve on a wood stove, and she had only Jesse and herself to cook for. She knew that she would do what she had to do to survive.

She brought the plate of cookies into the living room and sat them on a table. If the *posada* party wound its way around the high road to the upper part of Zacatecas Hill and stopped at her house for shelter, she would be prepared to invite them in. After all, she had something to offer them. This gift of cookies.

© Photo by Jim Lang

Part Three

You Do the Work

Migrant Workers © Photo by Becky Dickerson

where the poems are   **Christopher Cunningham**

I drew a man
with a big shit-feasting
grin
under a sun
with a flower
and
a bird.
next to it I wrote:
> dead
> broke
> but
> smiling
> in
> the
> sun.

one of my
co-workers
saw it and
said,
"hey that sounds
just like
my
life."

I said,
"that's poetry."

he smiled,
went outside
and
sat down
and
turned
his
face
to
the
sky.

Simple Pleasures   Buddy Struble

It's all the little things.
The alarm clock in the morning
Red eyes and disgust.
Construction on the way to work
Late
And the guy who never seems to find the speed limit.
The broken A/C in the car
but the heater still leaks
and the stereo doesn't work.
It's the red light you hit
Every time.
The phone bill
The house payment
The electric the insurance the child-support the gas the hate mail; you
owe, you owe
You owe
all at once.
The nights that seem too long.
The lines that are too long.
Too much time to think
too long.
Dirty socks and shirts and never enough time to do
anything.
A dog
lying in the ditch on a sweltering day
run over,
its legs stretched behind like so many useless days
panting in the sun.
Always feeling there's something undone.
Trash day
Flat tire
Eden after dark.

25 Down   **Buddy Struble**

Just now 25
and I talk about the old days
and how things have changed.
Just now 25 and already my knees talk aloud
when I tie my shoes
and my hands remind me of every hammered thumb
every abuse.
Already 25 and I take 5 pills a day
have a doctor
a lawyer
and an insurance premium.

Not 24 anymore
but still I don't drive a new car
or own my house
my career
or my future.
Almost 26
and my mother calls long-distance
to tell about my cousin
the lawyer
the concert pianist
married to a West Point grad,
my cousin 2 years younger
who just bought her own flat in New York.
My mother who wishes
I would get married.
Get serious.
Act my age because I'm almost 30.

Still 25 and watching Saturday morning Westerns
backing the Lone Ranger and Paladin
wondering where Will Sonnet really is
and how James West can ride a horse in those blue velvet pants.
Doing all this while only 25
and outside the whole world is mowing the lawn
and fighting about a monthly budget
fixing their mortgage rates and arranging babysitters.
At 25 all I arrange is my refrigerator.

At one-quarter of a century I have learned that history does
repeat itself
        repeat itself
and that if you unplug it
the phone doesn't wake you in the morning.

American Crawl   **Paul Allen**

Drowning in an oral surgeon's slough, Lake Martin.
To swim from the dock to the shallow bar, out to the flag
that warns lawyers their sons on slalom could break
a leg, and they would be obliged to toss thin Gimlets
overboard and rev twin Mercuries to the bone man's lot.

In this lake of families I forgot myself—the smokes,
the beer, the hours under the light, the hours
in strange towns looking for lights—and thought
I could make it. Didn't think.

Swim. My sister is doing o.k., saving her hair.
Her husband, who reconstructs mandibular joints,
is doing o.k. The boy from Stuttgart they swapped
their son for this summer is half there.
They are making it.

But I am not there, not even close. I see trees
over my elbow. The red bank tells me the dam
has given power to Eclectic and Wetumpka. The people
are saving their cukes and don't mind paying for it,
by God. So the man who controls the gates
has his orders. Somewhere around Kawliga down
the channel, the old river the Creeks lived on,
he is calling home and waiting for a light
to come on. He is resting his feet in a middle drawer.

I try it, to walk. A bad election. My foot
paws cold space like a white gelding counting his years
for a party in the mayor's yard. I am still in
too deep and sidle to the surface. Barely. Choke.
My privates are shrinking, and it's not funny.
I can't level off anymore. Like a slow low-rider
in Texas I know what I look like pulling
half of me, half of me dragging me down
to silt. The slender arms I wished for dry
have turned on me, like all prayers, into a horror
of slapping saplings falling on no meaningful water.

I learn now that giving up is not a matter of giving up.
There is paddling slowly for all I am worth,
tossing whichever arm wills toward air, dropping it,
kicking one leg, letting the other leg drag to a state,
to a kind of dream of paddling, of trees over my arm.
Even the real at the end of the dream is a dream—
my foot touching the feathers of tree limbs, snags,
then the thudding hump of land in a warm spot.

Such a let down coming out is, crawling to the three
who are laughing, leaning back in six inches on their elbows.
Like a lesson in perspective in Continuing Education art class,
I am looking down the roads of their spread legs.
The visitor from Germany offers a florescent
audacity at the vanishing point. I was kidding, wasn't I?
I was never in any real trouble, was I?
That was rich, the way I did and all. Rich.

I am (they tell me sunning), I am (in this world
of professionals), they can swear—my sister, my brother-in-law,
their exchanged student—oh Lord, like they have always said,
I am a hoot. I am a regular Goddamn riot.

The Waitress at the Waffle Shop   **Irene Sedeora**

Like a country singer
her voice twangs and
the scent of breakfast

infuses the air.
With her prattle she pours coffee
as cursorily as she mixed

a bloody Mary at Nick's,
the last place she worked.
In a voice full of grit

the waitress at the Waffle Shop
calls orders to the cook, then scatters
her life to the pair

perched at the counter.
"Last week I moved up here to have a life.
But I miss the beaches. I'm thirty-nine and

I never got married. It's just me and my dog."
The two aged birds munching waffles
nibble up
            every word.

Fault Lines   Michael Sterne

Mack thought the old man was drunk the way he shuffled through the door and eased onto a stool at the counter. He gave two hamburgers extra high flips, shook a fistful of French fries into a wire basket and set them to sizzling in the burnt brown oil before spitting his chew into the garbage and wiping his lips on his sleeve.

Rose had her back turned when he came in. She was explaining to some whiney tourists from Ohio how to get back to the interstate and hoping they didn't forget any of their bratty kids when they finally left. She turned around and noticed how the old man didn't grab the counter with his hands, just braced his palms against it and lowered himself gently onto the stool. *Arthritis or hemorrhoids*, she thought, and all that meant to her was that she was going to have to pour a lot of coffee, listen to somebody else's misery, and be lucky to count a fifty cent tip. She bused two tables and rang up a trucker's pigs 'n a blanket with a thermos to go before she brought him water and a menu, but the old man didn't complain. He just stared up at the tacky brown and tan cowboy prints hung over the cook's station and read the little cute-isms on the walls like the ones that said "longhorns that-a-way" and "sidesaddles this-a-way" pointing the way to the restrooms.

She slipped out the back door while he was looking at the menu and picked up the butt of a cigarette she'd laid on the gas meter outside. The wind was blowing hard out of the north and its cold touch slipped up the run in her stockings like a soldier's hand. *It's gonna snow tonight*, she thought. She fumbled around in her pocket until she found a butane lighter with a family crest on it that wasn't hers. She struck it. The flickering light lit up her bony face like a glow-in-the-dark Halloween mask. She snapped the lighter shut with a practiced flip of her wrist, took a deep drag on her cigarette, and let the smoke trickle off her lips like a honky-tonk love song. When she came back inside Mack had the burgers and fries under the heat lights.

"I told you no cheese," she said.

"Like hell you did" he replied. He had his sleeves rolled up and he was picking the scabs off a new tattoo of a cobra coiled menacingly on the inside of his left arm. He was a walking mural, but the snake was a first. He was hoping it would hide the tracks and collapsed veins of twenty-five years of heroin use. His other tattoos were mostly naked women with swords or fantastic fire-breathing dragons. His neck was emblazoned with an eagle-crowned swastika. The funny thing was, he was born Jewish.

Rose elbowed her way past Mack and through the kitchen door into the restaurant, ambling down the counter to where the old man waited. He'd folded his menu and laid it down in front of him; the universal sign, *I'm ready*.

"Coffee?" she asked.

"Black" he replied.

The old man's hands shook with tremors and Rose stared until he looked away. He folded them like haystacks on the counter but that didn't help, so he buried them in his lap. Deep furrows like the arroyos running through the badlands marred his face. He was crisscrossed with more fault lines than California.

She turned with less enthusiasm than a merry-go-round at a county fair and picked up a pot of rendered down coffee that would wake the dead and embalm them all at the same time. She held it in her right hand and felt around underneath the counter with her left for a clean cup. She looked up and the old man was leaning across the counter very close to her face. She could feel his breath on her eyelashes. The veins in his eyes stood out like roadmaps, bits of yesterday clung to his teeth like the memory of a bad dream. She could see every speck of the three-day's growth of brown and gray beard coming up like the dry weeds and frost she would find in her yard at two in the morning when she got off work. His skin had a pallid tint, a study in yellow, his jaundiced eyeballs, the nicotine stains on his lips that dribbled down his chin. It reminded her of the urinal in the men's room she hadn't cleaned yet. She poured his coffee.

He had a black hat that wasn't a cowboy hat, just a shapeless old bag of felt that kept the rain off his head and the shit out of his hair. It had plenty of use, too, she thought. *If I had a truck or a dog that old I'd put it to sleep.* "What'll ya have?" she asked.

"Just coffee."

She wrote out the check and slipped it under his cup before he could change his mind.

Mack slapped the bell, shouted, "Order up!" and she pulled the plates from under the heat lamps. He had scraped about half the cheese off the burgers. The fries hung over the edge of the plates like beach towels and sweated oil like Yankee tourists. *I can't serve this crap*, Rose thought, but she did anyway.

The Ohio man danced like a puppet in front of the cash register. Rose punched the numbers of his credit card into the box wrong and had to do it over again while he scowled and looked at his watch. She pictured him dressed in a sailor's suit doing a jig like Popeye, but that only made her think of a sailor she knew once in San Diego. He promised to be faithful, but the cafe didn't take checks anymore, either, so she imagined him like one of those ghetto blacks dancing when there wasn't any music. His wife walked out of the bathroom with her kids in tow and shot Rose a sideways look that said *If I ran over you on the highway, I'd wash my car first and call for help later*. What did she care? Her kids opened about fifty ketchup packages and smeared them all over the table. "Y'all drive safe now, you hear?"

On one wall hung a clock that had a cowboy in the middle waving pistols with both hands; an Indian crouched behind every hour. A Blackfoot speed freak on a Harley Davidson whacked it with a baseball bat one night and smashed the glass, but old Mel, the owner, ran out of the office with a sawed-off shotgun swearing he'd blow him straight to hell if he ever set foot in here again. It wasn't even ten o'clock.

At midnight Sheriff Bunson would come in for coffee and pie, his face blown-up like a drowned cow, his grimy olive uniform stinking of sweat like a greasy nickel. He'd drape his fat ass over his favorite stool, the same one where the old man sat slurping his coffee. Everybody knew he took bribes from over limit truckers and speeding salesmen and once asked Rose if she'd spread her legs for him when she complained because he impounded her car for breaking down on the highway. Hey, a girl's gotta work.

She pinched a butt out of an ashtray and headed for the kitchen again, but the college kids who ordered the burgers with no cheese cut her off. "I can't eat this," one of them complained, prodding the soggy fries like they might be sleeping and not dead. "My burger's cold," griped the other. He had an annoying squeaky voice and thick black glasses like a history professor.

They had a girl with them who wouldn't eat anything because she was a vegetarian and knew how to choose good restaurants. She had long auburn hair that hung down over her shoulders like a gasoline spill. "Let's go," she said. She wore a tight white muscle shirt that said PHISH in black letters on the front and no bra. Her pointy brown nipples looked like they might chew their way through like weasels.

I had tits like that once, Rose thought, and she slowly stroked the hair back from her temple. In fairy tales they made jewelry out of princess's hair, but like the Sierras, if there was gold there once, there's just ghost towns now.

The kids laid a buck down for their coffee and walked out.

Rose went out back and smoked the cigarette while the storm clouds ate the mountains west of town and the stars overhead and all her dreams. Little flecks of ice stung her face even though the clouds were not full overhead yet. The cigarette was menthol, too. *Just my luck* she thought.

Mack was no where to be found and Rose was sure he was drinking again. They had tried being lovers for a while but she couldn't stand the smell of work all the time. Besides, he kept having dreams he was in prison and Rose was afraid he would kill her in her sleep. She would die and never know the reason.

She thought the old man skipped out on his tab, but he had slid down the counter to eat the reject burgers the kids dropped in the bus tray. She bucked through the kitchen doors and turned on him like a rodeo bull, but he hung over the tray like a stray dog and she though he might bite if she came too close. He'd left his hat on the counter and his gray hair hung down in slimy coils like snakes behind him. He had a black satin trucker's jacket on with a bug-eyed man on the back with wrenches in his hands and the words Pervis Service stitched in red letters arching across his shoulders. It occurred to her that the jacket was stolen.

They had coyotes come down from the hills after the dumpsters like the rest of the bums and truckers, desert rats and crack whores who descended on the café on their way to Las Vegas. Old Mel put out poison sometimes, but mostly he didn't care. He kept a tarantula in a jar on his desk and when he was drunk enough he would bring it out and let it crawl on his face. He liked scaring kids and city girls. The rest of the time he holed-up in his office like Jesse James, drinking and counting his money, watching the goings-on through a peeling one-way mirror.

The old man finished his burger and turned around. His pants were dirty like he'd lived in them for a year, and his boots had soles once, too. "I ain't got no money," he said.

What did she care? In a couple of hours Sheriff Bunson would come in leering like a rat trap and when the snow got bad jumpy truckers would crowd the booths and drink endless pots of coffee and count the hours to Dallas. Mack might sneak up behind her, his breath like diesel exhaust, reeking of whiskey and cough syrup, and slip his hand up her skirt for the umpteenth time until she told him *no* and then he would go off and sulk like lizards under the rocks. Every day her face pulled a little further apart until no amount of make-up could hide the cracks and she was sure it was just a matter of time 'til the whole thing damn split right down the middle. "Just get out" she said.

The old man shuffled out the door with hat in his hands and his tail between his legs like winter leaving. Outside the snow began to fly for real, but Rose was sure some softhearted trucker would stop and be glad for the company, at least as far as Phoenix. Mack dropped a dish in the kitchen and it shattered like a windshield, like a wreck on the highway, like childhood. Rose wondered what hotels and bars and trucker's cafes might buzz to neon back east, if the air was really sticky, what frogs sounded like when they fucked under a full moon, and how it might feel to bleed young blood again.

By morning, snow would drift high as the hubcaps on a Peterbilt. It fell fast, now, big flakes tumbling down, and she had a sudden vision of a young girl dancing in the backyard of a queer little pink stucco cottage in Sacramento, laughing with her grandmother, catching snowflakes on her tongue. The old woman was bent like a vineyard under a crown of white, her brown hands bare to the cold, wrinkled like raisins. Rose wore wooly gloves, black and roomy like an old Pontiac. The world was her enchantress that night. She caught snowflakes like fairy's wings and marveled at their perfect symmetry. "Look!" she cried, over and over again, "Oh look!"

The old man was gone, his memory a crooked set of tracks leading off into the night. A line of trucks appeared on the highway, braked and banked, their wipers flopping like buzzard's wings, tires crunching gravel underneath. Rose stepped outside and listened to the diesels idle, the hiss as drivers set their brakes. She held out her hand on instinct but the snow swirled out of reach. "Hey, Mama" some smart-ass jake-jockey called, but Rose turned east like a night blooming weed. Somewhere she heard that no two flakes were alike, and she wondered how it could be they were different, every one that ever fell.

Migrant Workers, Ohio © Becky Dickerson

Fly Away   Jonathan Hayes

On the corner playing blues,
plugged into the afternoon.

She thumb-plucks bass, and sings about Chicago.
His fingers strum dark rhythms on a beat-up guitar.

Taking their earnings to Tad's Steaks, drinking cheap red wine,
and burying their forks and hunger in sirloins.

One day he climbs onto the amp, awkward but feeling good.
A harp player's jamming with them today, swaying and wailing away.

The crowd gathers, their minds, ears and eyes full of the blues.

Up on the amp he dances a sluggish red wine shuffle.
He's forgotten what fills the busker's belly.

He's singing an orchard song: a six-foot, hundred-seventy-pound
heart, cooked well done, and not served until the apple is

picked.

Car Broke Down   Dave Roskos

I caught a bus
to the Bricktown
Barnes & Noble
& called my brother
for a ride.
waited an hour
drinking coffee
& reading the beginning
of *1919.*
opened up The Outlaw
Bible of American Poetry
in the poetry section
to check if my poems
were still in it,
as a way to console
myself
& feel like less
of a loser.
It helped a little bit.
My first anthology—
got paid 20 bucks
& 2 copies.
I'm grateful,
don't get me wrong,
but the irony
of not being
able to buy
that copy
of *1919,*
& being in one
of the books
in that store,
kinda got
to me.

Sundae   **Irene Sedeoro**

Something sensual
the way he spoons
ice cream, the youth

behind the counter.
Something naughty,
the way he pours

warm chocolate,
and jets the cream.
Something fiery

the way his knife
halves a cherry.
"Enjoy," he says,

      with a wink.

Bad   Wanda Coleman

night at the taco house
he came in to rob the place
the waitresses were flush fear and tears
the guys sat around yammering
what he was doing caused some kind of disruption
he beckoned. i went over to his corner
he put the gun to my head, said "empty the register"
the kiss deep hard cold against my temple
there was a click sound
if i move sudden i'm dead, i thought
and if i hesitate this clown might off me
and so i said, "shoot motherfucka or quit wasting my time"
there was surprised silence
then everyone broke into strained laughter
"it's a joke," he said, "you didn't cry like the other girls"
and there were slaps on the back and
cracks about my ice cool
and from that day till the day i quit
everybody kept their distance

Newcastle Bar & Grill   **Thea S. Kuticka**

Across the street, a second-hand store displayed gold purses
and a man sold Avon after-shave bottles shaped like Model Ts.

He tried to sell one to me each time I went in,
even though I was too young to buy cologne for a man.

Summer afternoons, the carpenters walked down to the bar
for a drink and to watch my mother in her cork heels

as she tended to the after-five crowd. Her pockets filled with tips,
quarters spilled from her purse when she pulled out her keys,

and dimes sparkled in the gravel that lined our drive,
but we were still poor, and she was still a single woman

impressed by the man who sat at the bar with his red
Camaro parked out front. The cash drawer sang with change

when she gave it a final tap with her hip at the end of her shift.
She plunked a Shirley Temple down at my table with a half smile

reserved for patrons who didn't tip and gave me a handful
of thin mints hugged in foil. I savored the warm chocolate,

watched the gold purses spark across the street as the Camaro's
headlights lifted out of their sockets for the long drive home.

Espresso Jerk   Thea S. Kuticka

> —*Fair as a star, when only one*
> *Is shining in the sky.*
> —Wordsworth

This ache in my wrist, deep down to the tendons is testament
to the many shots I pulled, the grinds I tapped. Six a.m.,
I dropped the coffee cart counter down, turned on the grinder,
and waited for the sober ones, the workers, to queue up

for their first shot of the day. The vets from the VA hospital,
the computer programmers down the street, all so patient.
They knew how to stand in line and keep their feet dry
in the Oregon rain. The sound of milk under the nozzle

and the thick foam rising in my hands warmed their hearts.
The purple-haired teens with babies, the gothic poets,
the man who used to masturbate behind the cart while I
rolled lemons, where are they now? I hold my government

issued list of retirement points in my hand and I can see
that I'm worth more dead than alive. At twenty-four,
I thought getting paid under the table was a good thing,
as long as a mocha was steaming in Levi's hands in exchange

for a rail-flattened penny and my boss was losing money.
Mona, who pulled wet bills out of her trench coat's deep pockets
had told me I was an idiot. She was a loving insult, but she watched
out for me, shadowing me when I walked home late at night.

One morning, she finally accepted a free coffee,
then walked into the tallest building on campus, smoked
a cigarette in the men's bathroom, and leaped the seven floors
to the pavement, leaving her body to all those educated people.

For a moment, Mona was genderless in her star-lit fatigues
as she flew past the library's façade, the faces of scientists and poets,
presidents and politicians. She knew that we are worth more
dead than alive, that the masses would bring roses.

Bowling Alleys   Victoria Rivas

Sonny worked at the bowling alley
back when they ran on boy power. He
sat on a narrow beam of wood between
alleys. Balls barreled down toward his perch,
crashing pins left him a bit deaf by
the time the evening shift was over.

Twice each frame he would leap down, replace
live pins in the rack, sweep the dead ones
away, toss the ball down the return,
lower the rack. Sometimes a stray pin
would hit him. They hurt, left bruises. It
was dangerous work, but it paid well

and it impressed the girls who bowled there.
Sonny runs the bowling alley now.
A computer sets pins and keeps score.
Video game noise annoys him. Kids
with weapons frighten him. He wishes
he could impress the girls who bowl there.

Nocturnal Birds   John Cottle

To a man at the bottom of life, there is more to look up at—more to see. And less to lose. Trivial pleasures lie within easy grasp, unplundered by other hands reaching constantly upward in quest of grander prizes. At thirty years, Ronnie Arceneaux was looking up at all creation with a storm on his back. In better times, he would not feel the silent thunder rumbling his days or smell the dry lightning infecting his air. And he would not need her to soothe the edges of his discontent or to raise him above his anxious fears. He would not need her to do any of those things for him.

O'Connor's Garage in July. The three bay doors gaped into the scalded afternoon. Outside, lazy platoons of Johnson grass drooped in the swelter, flagged thirstily at sun-blanched fenceposts. Pecan trees bowed groundward, pushed by the slow breath of summer. A faded asphalt ribbon meandered into the horizon like a drunken peddler and a torrid humidity hung in the air think as gumbo. Birds flew slow or not at all.

She appeared along the roadside as if earth had spilled her there— no mere pilgrim traveling through the landscape, but a living piece of the afternoon, infused with the terrain through which she passed—and it was as if the continuity of time and space and proportion depended upon her presence within them at that very moment. Heatwaves seeped from the pavement and bent the distance beyond her and the honeysuckle vines that spanned the barbed-wire fencing waved slow-motion ripples in her wake. Her face was round as a pie, her skin of that rough, tawny hue that confessed of life under an Alabama sun. Rusted-ginger hair spilled in dirty tangles, curling upward below her jaw and roughly assuming the circularity of her face. She was of average height and of a bulky, corpulent build, and the stiff posture of her upper body seemed a mocking contrast to the gentleness of her countenance. A handbag road her shoulder, suspended by a thick leather strap, and in her hand, a small brown paper sack dangled insignificantly from the end of her stout arm. Her smile was carefree emptiness, her motion, unworried.

Hulking, redheaded, Claud O'Connor leaned against the door's edge, measuring the girl's approach. Across from him stood a ladder, carefully positioned within the threshold, and atop it, a boy wearing a striped workshirt, damp with a day's sweat. In the boy's hand was a power screwdriver and over his chest was patched the inscription, "Biles Overhead Doors." O'Connor rammed the toothpick deep between his eyetooth and bicuspid as the screwdriver whirred. Turning abruptly inside, he surveyed the cars and repair work scattered across the garage floor and the men engaged with it. He studied each job, nodding at the open car-hoods as if counting money soon to be banked. Then he turned to the boy.

"You go'n be through with that damn thing before six o'clock or'm I gonna have to stay here with you all damn night?"

"I'm go'n be done in half-an-hour, Mr. O'Connor," said the boy, unruffled.

"Not at the rate your slow ass is moving, you ain't."

"Half-an-hour, Mr. O'Connor."

O'Connor stepped through the door, flipped away his toothpick and spat a brown strand of tobacco juice to the pavement. "I don't mean for you to go rushing through with no half-assed job now. I gotta be able to lock that goddamn thing when we all go home."

"It'll lock for you when I'm done with it."

"I'd hate to have to sue Arnold Biles if somebody come in here tonight and stole me blind because that door wouldn't keep em out."

"Ain't nobody coming through this door without a key, wunst it's locked."

O'Connor looked back to the girl. She had just reached the edge of the parking lot. Her hand rose in a friendly wave and he returned the greeting. "Somebody tell Ronnie lunch finally got here," he shouted toward the back of the garage. Then, looking at the sack she carried, "You might as well just feed him supper now. Late as you are with that."

"The Lord knows I couldn't help it," she sighed. "That Janie Carlisle done gone off to Montgomery and forgot all about me setting there with her mama. And Miz. Merle, weak as she's done got, she can't be left alone without me knowing when Janie's coming back. So in she finally comes, two hours late, and then I have to wait on her to run me home cause I don't have no car. Then I have to walk here with his lunch. The Lord knows I couldn't help it."

"You need to get Ronnie to get you a car."

"You know he don't make money enough to get me no car, Mr. O'Connor."

O'Connor let go a deep laugh. "He makes a hell of lot more than what he's worth. And don't go trying to deny it either."

"Whatever it is, it ain't enough for him to get me no car with."

O'Connor took the round plug of tobacco from his mouth and hurled it over the parking lot and into the weeds by the roadside. He took a pouch of Red Man from his hip pocket and began cramming the leaves into his mouth. "Miz. Merle done hung on for longer than I ever give her."

"Sure has been a slow and cruel cancer," she said. "Be a blessing when she passes on."

"You'll have to get you another job then."

"Won't be hard. Somebody's all the time calling me, needing a sitter."

O'Connor turned back to the garage and called out again, raising his voice over the hubbub of clinking tools and idling engines. "Ronnie! Squirrel's here and got something for you."

A tall, solidly built man with thick glasses and a heavy moustache looked up from under an open hood. His face and hands were smeared with streaks of black grease. The glasses stretched his vacant brown irises into a pair of misformed orbs, possessed of neither rhyme nor grace. He caught sight of the girl standing in the doorway and put down the silver socket-wrench.

New Iberia, Louisiana, had not been a big enough place for Ronnie Arceneaux to hide. Five years ago he had climbed into the rusted-out pickup with his itinerant great-uncle at the wheel and left his native city in the middle of night, bound for Atlanta. He had just turned twenty-five and he was on the run. The felony assault warrant had been sworn out by the pregnant girl's irate father who could not abide the notion that anyone named Arceneaux, let alone one with the mind of a ten-year-old, had fathered him a bastard grandchild. And so Arceneaux had been caught up in a matter of honor in a world where matters of honor were settled with fists and two-by-fours, and when the violence broke out, it was Arceneaux who had quickly seized the upper hand. When the dust had settled and the blood had clotted, the father had little more than the strength necessary to crawl to the nearest telephone and call his friend, the chief deputy with the Iberia Parish Sheriff's Office. Arceneaux knew enough to pack his belongings quickly.

They made it as far as Springdale, Alabama, where the truck and the uncle gave out together. The truck got towed to a junkyard and the uncle taken to the local hospital where he coughed up a week's worth of blood in two days before making a graceless exit to the next world. Atlanta became no more than a stale plan, two hundred miles to the north and east.

O'Connor soon crossed paths with the luckless stranger and, having immediate need of extra hands and a fondness for a Cajun accent, set him up in the shabbiest of his five shabby rental houses—one within walking distance of the garage. Arceneaux was slow to learn, but the tasks of a mechanic's helper required little insight, and the cost of his muscle, from O'Connor's standpoint, was a square bargain.

Despite his slow-wittedness, Arceneaux proved reliable help, and his life soon settled into one of routine and repetition. Although a loner by nature, his persistent daily treks to and from the garage attracted the curiosity of several of the townspeople and he found himself the object of more charity and invitations to Sunday church services than met with his own idea of comfort. He had not the manners or finesse to refuse these random kindnesses and consequently, he became an unwilling, visible fixture to most of the Springdale populace.

The girl he now eyed over the tools and transmission parts and piston rings and scatter of the garage floor had been sent to him six months ago by O'Connor while he was bedridden with an extended case of flu. She was known to most of Springdale's 1200 inhabitants only as Squirrel, few of them ever having heard of the name, Mary Garmon. She lived in a singlewide house-trailer near Arceneaux and supported her sparse existence with various odd jobs, most of which involved caring for the sick. She had brought him groceries and medicine and even done a little cooking and laundry, and when he got over the flu, she continued to do the same things for him and he did not complain. Nor did he complain when she came to him one evening and slowly peeled away his blue work jumpsuit and then her own clothing, and took him to bed and lay with him until morning, nor even when she brought her toothbrush and the small box of toilet articles to leave for the convenience of regular weekend visits. As he watched her now through the stir of dust off the concrete floor, bringing the small sack that he knew contained a baloney sandwich and a can of sardines, he did not see the thick flesh that hung from her arms or the coarseness in her skin or the chestnut flush of her picketed teeth, but looked instead upon an approaching comfort—a hard-used angel bearing common blessings—and a smile came up under the grime of his face as she waded toward him through the clutter.

"You late wi' dat, ain'cha?"

"Mr. O'Connor says you need to get me a car. Then I won't be counting on the mercy of Janie Carlisle to haul me around everwheres."

She handed him the sack and they retired to a corner of the garage and sat at a small wooden table. He unwrapped the sandwich and opened the sardines while she spread napkins over the grime of the tabletop. He offered her a sardine, which she took and ate all in one piece.

Morris Cole, the new mechanic, slithered underneath the Ford Taurus parked nearby, his back against a rolling-board. Arceneaux did not like Morris Cole, and he liked being indebted to him even less. He knew Cole had been watching him for weeks and he had felt the menace in his quicksilver eyes and the sense of impending trouble those eyes always drew through his nerves.

It was soon after Cole began working at the garage, that the games had started. O'Connor would lock the doors, a wooden bench was turned on its edge, the dice came out, and money went down on the floor. The others showed him how. Sometimes he picked up the piles of cash and sometimes he reached for the money only to have his arm grabbed while another hand swept it away, but he always finished with less than he started. The last time, he had it lost all and they let him sign pieces of paper so he could keep playing and as the dice kept banging against the bench, he kept signing the papers until O'Connor made him quit. Then Cole would show up every Friday with his friend Thayer, and when the paychecks were handed out, Thayer would cash them for the men at discount, and Cole would be there wanting money from Arceneaux. There had been arguments over how much Cole could have and Cole had made threats, and then he had felt the storm within him that had lain five years dormant. Now as he eyed Cole sliding around under the Taurus, he felt the storm gathering, felt the weight of its building danger and sensed that its growing surge would sweep him up within itself and there would be nothing that he could do to prevent it.

He finished the sandwich and she ate the last of the sardines, and then she went to the front and waited for him, joking with the workers until closing time. She bought them Cokes from a machine and then O'Connor let down the new door and locked it for the night. She put the Cokes in her handbag and they set out together. The sun was low in the sky and the thick air still held the day's heat, and the sweat came quickly as they walked. They took the dirt road toward Harley Newman's hayfield, and when they reached the familiar cluster of mimosas, they crossed the runoff ditch and he held the barbed-wire apart for her to step through, and then he followed her into the field. They crossed the field to the pole barn where they were out of sight of the road and sat on the firm ground underneath the shelter of its tin roof, looking west into the setting sun. The field sloped downward before them to a creek, and beyond the creek were woods of oak and hickory with a smattering of poplar and pine, and the star-like leaves of sweetgums were mixed among them all. They drank the Cokes and he threw his empty across the creek and into the woods, and she scolded him for it and put hers back into the handbag. She sat close to him and they did not speak, but he drew comfort from her nearness and from the hand that stroked his back in repeating circles. As the sun worked its way down through the trees, the sounds of dusk rose out of the ground, the crickets and katydids crying to the approaching darkness, then a woodwind of nightbirds, a trio of whip-poor-will notes, and he felt the day ebb into a sea of choruses that thrummed from the living earth like a heartbeat, and the blood in his veins ran smooth and even, and the storm was far away.

Friday afternoon came and Thayer was there at the garage door, taking the paychecks and handing out cash. O'Connor stood at the far end of the parking lot, talking with a man from the bank. The banker was writing in a notebook as O'Connor pointed out things about the building. Arceneaux looked at his check. One hundred twenty-two dollars after deductions for rent and taxes. Thayer held out a fifty and two twenties.

"Ain't enough," said Arceneaux.

"The shit you say. A man's entitled to an honest commission, ain't he?"

"You ain't no honest man."

"Now don't you go insulting me, Cajun boy," said Thayer. "If you don't want my services, you can just wait till Monday and take it to the bank."

"Ninety ain't fair. Last time it'a hundred."

"Cost of living's done gone up since last time, Cajun boy. Ain't you ever heard of inflation?" Thayer pulled a five out of his pocket. "Here. Here's ninety-five. Take it now or go to the bank on Monday."

"He ain't got till Monday." Cole's voice was flat—portending urgency. "He owes it tonight."

Arceneaux turned away from Thayer and took a step toward the door. Cole stepped directly into his path. Cole was perhaps a couple of inches shorter than Arceneaux and a good twenty pounds lighter. He had jet-black hair that stopped just before his shoulders and framed the hard-edged features of his lean face. His sleek, muscular build suggested a controlled quickness—as if he could have been a matador in another life. Arceneaux looked at him and felt the boiling inside. He stepped to his right to skirt around Cole, but Cole matched his movement and remained between him and the door.

"Don't you think about leaving here owing me money, you son of a bitch," said Cole.

"I pay you Monday. Monday I go to the bank."

"You go'n pay me tonight, you goddamn half-wit. Now sign that check and give it to Thayer and get the money."

"I going home. You get out my way now."

"Oooh! Cajun boy's talking tough now, ain't he," mocked Thayer.

"Why don't I just go home with you, then," said Cole. "Get me a little of that stuff you like so much."

"Wha'chew talking bout?"

"Your ugly little Squirrel. I bet that's some good stuff, ain't it Ronnie? Gotta be good for you to hang around with something ugly as that."

"You shut up bout her."

"You just take me on home with you, and I'll trade out your debt for a little of that pussy. How'ed that be?"

"I done said you shut up bout her now." He felt the muscles tightening and the swells rising from his stomach and he knew that something wild was loosening inside of him.

"I do believe you done gone and got him pissed off, Morris," said Thayer.

"You pissed off at me Ronnie?" Cole stepped closer. "Now why would you be pissed off at me? You the one that owes *me* money." He reached forward and put his palm against Arceneaux's chest and gave him a slight push. "You sign that check and give it to Thayer there so's you can pay me. Either that, or you fix me up with a little of that Squirrel pussy you like so good and maybe I'll forget…"

Arceneaux's swing barely grazed Cole's cheek. The force of the punch left Arceneaux reeling off balance and Cole was quick to take advantage. Three rapid blows to the head and Arceneaux was staggering backward, his glasses on the concrete floor. Cole kicked them hard toward the other end of the garage. Arceneaux got his legs back under him and the two men faced off, circling in the garage door, dark blood trickling from a cut above Arceneaux's eye.

The booming anger of O'Connor's voice brought all motion to sudden stillness. He moved swiftly for a man of his size. His hands landed hard against Cole's chest and then Cole was against the wall with his feet six inches from the floor and O'Connor was nose to nose with him. The other men backed away; one went to retrieve Arceneaux's glasses.

"What the hell you think your doing?" shouted O'Connor.

"I'm just trying to collect my money." His voice quivered. "He swung at me first. Ask any of them."

O'Connor released his grip, but did not back away. "I don't allow that kind of collecting to go on here."

"He's the one swung at me. And he owes me fair and square. You seen him lose it to me."

"How much you figure he owes you."

"Hundred and fifty. It's an honest debt. I was just trying to collect and the crazy bastard swung at me."

O'Connor pulled a roll of bills from his pocket and peeled off a hundred and a fifty and stuffed them into Cole's shirt-pocket. "That oughta make things even. Now get whatever tools you brought in here with you and get your ass away from here. I don't want to see you anywhere around here again, you hear."

"Fine." Cole's voice broke slightly. He brushed his chest where O'Connor had lain hands on him and paused, as if trying to collect himself. "Just give all my work to your half-wit there and let him finish with it."

"Don't worry yourself about it. We'll get it done without you." Then, turning to Thayer, "And you too. Clear your ass outta here and don't ever let me catch you around here again either."

Thayer's mouth drew into a tight smile that matched his smirking eyes. "And good evening to you too, Mr. O'Connor," he nodded.

Cole threw a few wrenches and sockets into a small red toolbox and climbed into Thayer's pickup. They had not left the parking lot before O'Connor found Arceneaux. He was wiping off his glasses on his shirttail, then holding the scratched lenses up to the light and wiping again.

"You need to be more particular about who you get yourself in debt to."

"Them two ain't honest. They try to cheat."

"Well, now you owe me another hundred and fifty. So there's one more deduction from your paycheck. You go'n soon be working for nothing, at the rate you're going."

"I glad he gone. He ain't no count."

"You had no damn business playing dice to begin with. I oughta have put a stop to it. Now I gotta go find me another mechanic."

"It better he gone. He ain't no good. He go'n cause bad trouble."

O'Connor pulled a rag from his hip pocket and began dabbing it over the blood on Arceneaux's face. "You better get on home. Squirrel's gone be wondering what happened to you."

Arceneaux adjusted the glasses on his nose and crossed the parking lot. At the road, he stopped and looked back at O'Connor standing in the big doorway with the garage's interior glowing behind him. Their eyes locked for a brief instant and Arceneaux's mouth opened as if he were about to speak, and then it closed again and he turned back to the road and began to walk.

He took the dirt road and headed for the mimosa trees, and when he reached them, he stepped over the ditch and made his way between the strands of barbed wire and into the field. He found her sitting under the pole barn. The sun was beyond her and low in the sky and the long shadows of the trees stretched out toward her and covered the creek in their shade. She sat silent at his approach and only turned to look at him when he had sat down beside her. Then he felt her hands against his face and she was wiping above his eye with a white handkerchief and when she took it away, there were dark round splotches on it. He felt the turning within him and felt the fear of what she had discovered upon the handkerchief and of how he would have to tell her of it. He looked away, but she placed a hand on his cheek and gently turned his face back toward hers. She did not speak, but the questions were there within her eyes and he felt their challenge, and lacking the fortitude for response, he did not make effort to answer, but sat still at her side in the crescendo of dusk and together they listened.

The summer wore on, sultry and unrelenting. Then September came in as hot as July and the men at the garage talked of the heat and the older ones argued over when a south Alabama summer had ever burned hotter. Arceneaux's life fell back into a patterned existence—a routine orbit among things familiar and common. His seas had calmed and the wind blew soft within him, as though spent of its passion, and he felt himself adrift in a welcomed normality.

There came a Friday in late September when the oppressive summer had begun to wane and the advancing dusk encroached steadily, day by day, upon the afternoon. When he left the garage, the west was mottled with bands of blood-orange and sky. As he walked the roadside, a cubby of quail burst from the brush before him and took wing in the failing light and he paused to watch their flight. It was full dusk when he reached the dirt road and the half-moon was ringed in mist. Lights from a distant farmhouse shimmered over the breadth of a cotton field and the white bolls caught its light and that of the moon too, and they were as the reflections of stars on a vast and calm lake.

He did not hear the footfalls until he was a hundred yards onto the dirt road, and when he first thought he heard them, he turned and saw nothing, so he kept to his path. When he heard them again, he knew he was being followed. He turned and looked into the darkness behind him and saw the shadowy form frozen against the night. He called out to it and there was no answer or movement and he stood looking into the form and feeling the old winds rising inside him and he began to tremble. He took a step toward it and it likewise began moving toward him. Then the familiar voice of Cole came against his ear and the storm within him gained.

"What you got hid out here, Ronnie boy?"

"Wha'chew want wi' me?"

"I wanna know what you hiding out here. Might wanna get me some of it myself."

"Ain't nothing here for you. You git on." He stood his ground while Cole advanced slowly.

"That ain't a very nice way for you to be talking to me, Ronnie. Not after you done cost me my job."

"I ain't cost you nothing. You jus' ain't no count, is why you ain't got no job."

"Listen at you, you half-witted son of a bitch. Telling me I ain't no count. Why you ain't worth the powder it'd take to blow your Cajun ass away and you telling me I ain't no count?"

"Jus' let me lone. I don't want no trouble."

"It's too late for that. You done caused me a bait of trouble and now it's fixing to cost you."

Arceneaux saw the vague outline of a club—saw it draw back to strike—and backed away quickly. The blow glanced off his chin and he fell to the ground. He scrambled to a squat and saw Cole coming toward him with the club drawn back and he covered his head with his arms. The blow landed full against his back and he absorbed its force and then rose quickly upward, coming in between Cole's arms. His hands went directly to Cole's throat and locked tightly around his neck. Cole struggled in vain to free himself and the club fell to the ground. As Arceneaux gripped tighter, he felt a softness in the neck, and the fury came whole within him and its strength bore into Cole's throat and the sounds of Cole's breathing became strained as the intake of clogged bellows. His fingers and thumbs pressed harder now and the thumbs found yet a softer spot below the larynx and they dug fiercely downward until no sound came from the constricted throat. The struggle within Cole's body ebbed away under Arceneaux's unrelenting grip. Still he did not release—could not release, because the storm was full within his hands and its savagery was boundless, and the limpness in Cole's body did not ease it, but drove it harder until finally the muscles of his thumbs and fingers gave way to exhaustion and let fall to the ground, the lifeless body of Morris Cole.

He stood over the body watching for any movement, his breath labored as an overfired steam engine. He pushed at the body with his boot, and still nothing. "Get up!" he yelled to the corpse. The storm was exploding now and its intensity choked him and his breath came in rapid wheezes. He grabbed Cole's shirt at the chest and pulled him to his feet and pled with all the force of his lungs for Cole to stand, but when he released his hold, the body dissolved into a pile at his feet. Again he raised Cole up and begged him to stand, but this time he felt the wilted emptiness in the flesh he held, and he knew the futility of his pleas.

He carried the body a few paces into a fallow field across the road from the cotton and let it fall to the ground among the weeds. Then he walked back to the road and continued down it in his previous direction. His foot kicked against something and he reached down and picked up the club—nothing but a dried hickory branch of a couple inches diameter. He hurled it with all his strength into the weeds of the untilled field, and the vines and briers swallowed it up and it became forever a part of the earth upon which it landed. He took deep breaths as he walked, hoping to control the roil that pushed from inside, and he ambled the road with wasted motion so that time and its passage might soothe the turmoil that coursed within him.

At the mimosas, he settled to the ground, his back against a fencepost, and looked into the night sky, distorted from the moisture in his eyes. Then he closed his eyes on the stars and rested his head against the post and filled his lungs with the pure night air. Images of chaos came upon him out of the darkness, visions of terror and pain, fragments of old fears and torments spinning randomly through his head and plundering his thoughts, people asking him questions in tongues he had no ear to hear, moving about him and behind him, their voices familiar echoes from his past but their words dissolving into hostile babble that he could not take into his head, demanding of him what he could not give them or even understand. He buried his face in his hands and felt a cool moisture come over his skin. He sat in that way for a length of time. When he opened his eyes the world he saw was quiet and the field spread out before him, cold and colorless in the moonlight. The path stretched out ahead, clear and familiar, and he made his way along it through the hay.

When he reached the barn, she was waiting, seated cross-legged with her back to his approach and looking into the woods where the sun had set. Then he heard it, the sound of night bubbling around them, coming to him as a different and unknown song. The rhyme of the crickets and groundbirds struck his ear at strange new angles and the resonance of the song filtered through him and mingled with his turmoil, and the melding of it all within him was an unstable mixture of solitude and misgiving—a transient state that could not sustain itself, but only drifted in and out of his consciousness like a windblown cloud. She stood to meet him and when he reached for her, she gave him her warmth and the life within her lips. They embraced one against the other, at home among creatures who shun the daylight—who assume earth's colors and burrow themselves into secret wombs to wake with the fall of darkness and fill the night with their song. The half-moon dripped its light over them and they stood there together within the richness of their moment and he traced the contours of her face with his callused fingers while they waited on the world and on all that it had left to bring them.

Mornings Outside the Boiler Room   **Amber Shields**

Six a.m. at Jefferson Junior High, three men
in blue shirts sitting on empty milk crates
put out there to air for the summer,
one man smoking a cigarette, all three drinking coffee
from styrofoam cups, watching the day dawn and thinking
those floors'll still be there when the sun's done risin'.

Larry and Jim   **Amber Shields**

Larry's up with the sun, at work by 6:30 and off by three,
home in time to coach baseball for his son's team,
or go out on a call with the Carver Fire Dept..
His is an unlikely blue-collar paradise:
wife, kids, home, and a '91 Ford pick-up—blue.

Jim drives in at 9AM in his shiny green Chevy.
It's equipped with four doors, power windows,
and all the practicality a good-looking,
single father like Jim could want.
When he returns from his week off
with stories about his road trip out west with his son,
I wonder if he doesn't wish he had a truck
like Larry's, except maybe in red.
In his thirty-six years he's stretched his horizons
like a rubber band, around college
and six years speaking Spanish in the Coast Guard,
but fact is, a rubber band is still a circle,
no matter what you stretch it around,
and he just can't see how he ended up here
with a blue shirt and a mop, working nights
and smoking pot behind the dumpster,
trying to forget that he always gets home too late
to play catch in the back yard with his kid.

Before the August Dawn

Trina S. Scordo

I ride my green Huffy
to an abandoned fabric factory
where Grandma worked
look for proof she was alive last night

I dig through concrete and cloth
climb stacks of plywood
next to a charcoal stone wall
demolished lathe and nails
a pile of brick and mortar
a splinter in my finger

I search for her
in black corner walls
smoke and chalk rise
broken bits of tile and steel
where she stood
stitching patches of blue and red

there is nothing
not a lock of white hair
a thick finger in a thimble
a slippered foot on a Singer
sewing machine peddle

raw blistered hands
mesh wire caught on my jeans
I ride home
pockets heavy with dust and copper
under a humid 4 AM moon
I am left with brittle pennies
on Grandpa's cold garage floor

Mr. Merckle   Trina S. Scordo

Mr. Merckle's denim jacket
smells of burnt lead and steel
calloused hands from the Secaucus auto plant
finger nails covered in soot
every afternoon spent under the hood
of a white '61 Impala

in front of his goldenrod aluminum house
kids play baseball
he is the official referee
never misses a pitch or a call

soiled Jersey accent
he answers questions
about a green anchor tattoo
on his forearm

at the corner of John and Catherine
he counts the number of American cars
parked in front of rows of red brick houses
gray trees in cracked tar

at night
under a dusty moon and rusted stars
he drinks cans of Schaefer beer
on his crooked wooden deck
hopes nothing will change

he wants forty hours a week
linking metal to metal
overtime on weekends welding
Caterpillar trucks
believes every inch of his steel kingdom
is solid like the dye-cast glow
of used car signs
on highway 46

Doubles   **Will Watson**

on a 16 hour shift
a double, as they say
it might well be possible
to die just before 7 am
without really noticing
and if you did your double
feeding heavy gauge
on the 54" temper mill
in hundred ten degree August
death will be something
that will occur to you
but i outstrip myself
beginnings are better
for i have walked into that wall
of heat and stench and noise
that is the north end in August
wilting with each step
safety glasses steamed on sweated nose
relieved Red Husiar as he slouched
his rail thin hip and hollow cheek
on the filthy feeder rail
noted he sprang wordless for his time
card, snapping it from Chet Peebly's fist
without breaking stride and i have
felt 3000 horsepower acquaint my spine
my skull my hands and feet with power
and with servitude to power
as i eyed the first dwindling coil
whose wraps unwound
toward its empty eye and toward
auto bodies and cans of peaches and a thousand unknown
forms and i have punched the feeder's bell
three shorts to tell Smitty or Dirty Red or Pollack One
or some boy roller no older than me
too young to have a nickname
yet, hey wake up we're bringing her down
and i, who was first Willy Boy and then Doc
would gouge the red speed-reduce
twist the tension rheostat lower now
lower just enough the strip neither rips

nor sags and certainly my eyes would snap
from my diminishing coil
to tension gauge to speed meter till she slowed
enough i could hit stop and did and leaped
twelve pound power shears first
to cut the buckling tin
and nobody has ever thrown a heavier butt
or had feet more sure on the greasy conveyer
and when the next coil shuffled in
i'd seize the head end
and stick it straight straight straight
into the feeder bars into first stand
no pinchers no scored rolls
no roll changes in eight hours
no down time, no sir, none
and i've done all this and more
fifty times from dusk to midnight
tasting oil in bologna scarfed standing up
eyes pricked for rough edges and stickers
that would blow both stands to hell
if i didn't catch them first
and i have missed them and lunged
for the e-stop, staggering
away in showers of shattered tin
lowering my eyes when Redneck Bobby
damned me for dope smoking fool
swearing he'd can me for three days w/out pay
and yet i've known too
the sweet flicker of north end fame
when Vinnie Savarese chalked
our record thousand ton turn, one
that still stood years after
i've heard tell
have known both cold free beer
slurped with men my father admired
on the carpet in the sweet cool
of the Super's suite at midnight
and the anguish of midnight and no relief
man and the promise of another night
of roaring steel on top of the first one
and have resigned myself
to not speaking below

a scream until after dawn resigned
myself to another four dozen tail ends
nine hundred tons and a narrowed soul
and all this has been mine
the skin of my life for years
perhaps the pith of it
too in those days and nights
when it seemed the soft hands
beyond the wire
must be getting enough sleep
to stay awake forever and
i have come through
and when not even Rudy Jania himself
could make me feed
a single minute more
have snapped my time
card, nodding yes into Red's amused
"They got your ass too, eh?"
and climbed the shivering stair
to my locker and a warm shower
that felt a little like holy water
on my bunched back and shoulders
and i have joined the other midnight men
no longer strangers, but my doubles
walking fast, faster with them
through the tin shear warehouse
across the loading bays
found my voice with them
burst aching into dawn with them
past blinking guards and barbed wire
toward our cars homes and sleep
our feet freed from steel
shank steel toe boots
stepping lighter and faster lighter faster
until it seemed
at the last
we were surely going to fly

Half

David Mason

"I take the shortcut in a wilting crosswind,
hauling half of someone's prefab house
through brown prairie that drinks the melting snow.
Three days ago I fit my hands around
better curves than this—and she half my age
and wanting me to stay at least till payday.
Then the call came. The way I jumped to work
you'd think I wanted money, her bullet eyes
drilling my back. That door she slammed behind me
damn near threw a hinge, but when I climbed
behind the wheel I half knew I was home.
Here nothing stands up to the wind for long,
the pronghorns all run off, the highway signs
pitched like crazy drunks, shot through with birdshot.
A gunbarrel road, Limon to Last Chance,
but this wrapped half a house catches the wind
and slows me something awful, otherwise
I'd push these eighteen wheels until they purred,
turn up Bob Dylan singing *Maggie's Farm*
and catch its other half in no time flat."

Day Labor   Mac Lojowsky

...Fairbanks, Alaska

Today I was handed a chainsaw
and ten cash dollars an hour
clearing forest for buildings.

Aspen, willow, spruce, birch,
young, old, thick and thin,
it all came down,
it all stacked up.

By quitting time,
I had cleared almost a half acre,
my slash pile stood ten feet tall.

There was one hundred dollars
in my pocket,
a dead forest at my feet.

The blood on my hands
was my own.

After Ginsberg   **Dave Roskos**

Easter Sunday 1999
Dwyer & Loring just left
spent the night
watching movies, talking,
smoked a joint on the roof around midnight.
read Allen Ginsberg
from *Cosmopolitan Greetings*,
    'After Lalon,' he advises:
"Allen Ginsberg warns you
  don't follow my path
          to extinction"
He, unhappy with fame route
        he had taken—
Honest enough to admit it,
so that others could learn
      from his mistake.

      Better to stay obscure?
   move furniture for a living?
    sweat of brow, literally,
          & ache of back?
sore legs growing muscular
  through busy summer season
    trudging with dressers,
      boxes, sofas, chairs,
pianos, appliances

                Up
            &
                Down
Stairs,

On & off
      trucks?
maybe —
          more honest than
              teaching –
          & as seasonal.

CA Redemption   John Olivares Espinoza

I'm tossing out my *Time*
Magazines and kitchen trash
And see a Mexican waist deep
(Or is it just waste deep?)
In the mouth of an orange dumpster.
He's wearing a green soccer jersey
The color of old lettuce leaves,
His player number is lucky seven
And maybe he had a nickname then,
Like *La Pata*, The Foot,
Maybe he played with my uncle?
Now he's ripping through
Plastic grocery bags,
Sifting through vegetable pudding,
Used tampons and condoms
Wrapped in toilet paper,
His chinos soaking in chicken grease,
On his aluminum hunt.
The thick smell of stale cola
Reminds me of recycling with Mom
Every other Saturday at Lucky's
When I was a kid:
Two cans for five cents,
And the vending machines
That sucked and crushed cans
Down to colorful hockey pucks,
And whose turn it would be to press
The blinking redemption button,
And watching the nickels and dimes
Pour like a metal rain
Inside a small slot.
I remember getting older
And embarrassed
For relying on recycling
To eat lunch.
So I left Mom alone,
Patiently emptying grocery bags
Full of soda cans
One by one.
The soccer player sees me

And quickly looks downward
At his feet and pride
Sinking among trash bags.
I tell him there's a few
Soda cans in my trash,
Walk back upstairs
To grab last night's Bud Light cans
And stale Little Debbie
Coffee cakes
To give him.
He's still there, stomping around,
And he accepts them
As he would a smile
On this Monday,
Martin Luther King's Day,
Not that it matters
Because the shrubs are freshly trimmed,
Which tells me the gardeners
Didn't get the day off,
Which means my Dad
Is putting in ten hours
Across the lawns.
The soccer player
Walks away
With a white plastic bag
Weighed down by
The worth of an empty six-pack:
A few hard-earned cents
That will preserve him
In the light of the world
For one more day.

Grass Isn't Mowed on the Weekends   John Olivares Espinoza

What first comes across your mind about the stocky
Mexican pushing a mower across your lawn
at 7 a.m. on a Saturday as the roar of the cutter
wakes you? Let me take a guess. "Why do they
have to come so damn early?" What do you make
of his flannel shirt missing buttons at the cuffs,
dethreaded at the shoulders, the grass stains around
his knees, the dirt like roadmaps to nowhere,
between the wrinkles of his neck? Let me take a shot.
"Dirty Mexican." Would his appearance lead you
to believe he is a border jumper or wetback
(you may take your pick) who hits the bar
top with an empty shot glass for the twelfth time
then goes home to kick his wife around like fallen
grapefruit lying on the ground? After the countless
years like grassblades this man has mowed, of trying
to dissolve stereotype, what good would you make
of this poem? First, the stocky Mexican isn't mowing
your lawn at 7 a.m. on a Saturday. He doesn't work weekends
anymore ever since he lost 1/3 of his route to laborers
willing to work for next to nothing. Second, he knows
better than to kneel on the wet grass because, well,
the knees of his pants will become grass-stained
and pants don't grow on trees, even here, close
to Palm Springs. Instead, after 25 years of the same
blue collar work, two sons out and one going in college,
rather than jail, and a small, but modest savings
in case he loses the remaining 2/3 of his work—no matter
how small and reluctantly the checks come in the mail,—
my father the stocky gardener, believes he firmly holds
his life in both hands like pruning shears, chopping
branches and blossoms, never looking downward,
as they fall to his feet in pieces, like the American dream.

Shane's Produce   Paul Allen

(Beginning with a line by Dietrich Bonhoeffer)

Here we have the raw material of tragedy.
A boy, presumably Shane, with an old woman
at their roadside stand after the summer shower
which came so suddenly, it simply was
and wasn't—left the road steaming in a clean sun.
Four lanes of lives stopped at the light.
The woman still holds a corner of the sheet
that says **Shane's Produce**. The one great gust
ripped their blue tarpaulin from its grommets,
folded it like a napkin and laid it across
the hood of the truck.
They are soaked through.
Shane stands empty handed.

Now, what can you make of that?

Can you make a story that does not make us cry?
Try. See what you can do before the light changes.
The wet boy of indeterminate age (and IQ),
the wet old woman, letters bleeding, and everything
covered with bits of chips and bark from the pines,
like cartoon pepper on a cartoon portion
on a cartoon giant's plate. Lovers oddly paired?
Perhaps school was too.... Or she is teaching
him the value of.... Or his parents have
(have not?).... Maybe they don't need
the money or the produce but need to watch
the cars go by, or they hope to help drivers
at the light pump up the sludge of charity
which has settled to the bottom of their lives.

But you see the problem.

Any facts beyond the fact of the two, any scenario
beyond the red-light's life in front of Wal-Mart
winds up breaking your heart,
doesn't it? Once anything touches this scene—
the slightest why or when or sin or lie or who

or laugh (or two) breaks through—
the whole thing washes down the road and floods the state.

It takes a better mind than mine, or cleaner soul,
to animate these people with something
other than trembling lips, a dry cry in the throat.
Try. Bring this to Good—without throwing your god
or gods into the mix—the old *deus ex machina*—
to make things come out lovely. (Probably
too much *ex machina* in all this as it is.)
Shards of glass in the kitchen whenever the train goes by,
chickens dead and head wounds, lovers in the lost and found,
piles, and smiles, and headaches, smelly pillows,
clots and burps and broken arms, a bent this or that
to be explained at camp, and AA and Amway
and Jesus and bennies and butt boils
and the person who painted the cars
and the person who made the paint
and the old woman's corns
and the boy-man's saint—
we cannot read or write the story of anyone
without our fingers stilled over the home keys.

At this light, the next light, the last light
such scenes appear complete, so neat they make
some of the biggest messes in the world.
Like this one on the side of the road.
And the road. And the world.

You Do The Work   Sandra Lee Stillwell

Dark skinned   brown eyed
   handsome man
you work the vineyard
grow the grapes
but do not own them.

   I glimpse your shyness
and smell the honesty in your sweat
you do the work
grow the grapes   make the wine.
We shake hands
and I feel your calluses
see the soil buried deep within your skin
I see the scars   the split fingernails
earned in years of hard work
years of adverse weather
you do the work
grow the grapes
but you do not own them.

   I taste the sweetness in the wine
colored burgundy
sparkling in summer sunlight
it is dull
compared to the glow   the glint
   the pride in your brown eyes
you do the work
you grow the grapes   make the wine

I fear   my friend
that the vineyard   the grapes
and especially the wine
may own you
as a child owns a parent
but never the other way around.

Anson   David Budbill

Anson was born on the place next door, half a mile away.

About ten years ago the university took part of the Boynton place for
taxes.
(The university, by the way, has been delinquent on the taxes ever since.)
Not long after that the Boyntons sold out, but Anson came back a few
years ago with a French wife and two sons to farm his home.
He rented from the owner, a chiropractor in California.
Anson sold out last spring.
The bank wouldn't loan him money for machinery
because he didn't own the place and because
the chiropractor wouldn't give him a long-tern lease.

Anson's gone.
Kicked off the place he was born on
By somebody he never met.

They were good neighbors. My boy and their boys
played together, rode their bikes up and down the road,
built forts in the woods, fished for trout in the brook,
gave each other courage to make it through a day at school.

Anson spread shit on our garden free of charge,
helped me draw my wood, used to take all three boys
on a sleigh behind his snow machine.
Marie took the boys to Morrisville to the movies.
She was pretty and alive. It was fun
to watch her move across a room.
We never visited all that much but they were good neighbors.

Anson busted his ass over there. It was his home
even if he did have to rent it. He busted his ass
and for nothing.

Everybody says the Boynton place is jinxed,
says nobody can make a go of it over there.
Anson could have if he'd had a break.
It's not the farm that's jinxed. It's farming.
Grain goes up, milk goes down.
The U.S. secretary of agriculture has deliberately

conspired against the family farm.
The name of the game in Washington is agribusiness,
huge consolidated farms big as Continental Can.
Down there they want the family farm to die.
They want fewer and fewer people
to have more and more money.

This is not my fantasy.
The Associated Press reported last week
that the secretary of agriculture admitted during a senate hearing
that he thought the family farm should be "phased out."

Here's the secretary again: "Farming isn't a way of life.
It's a way to make a living."
God forbid somebody should see his life and living
as the same thing. What are these idiot neighbors of mine
doing anyway thinking they should love their work?
Don't they know the end of work is money?

Listen, this isn't an issue doesn't concern you.
This issue is the death knell
for what little anarchistic independence is left.
It is oligarchy's fanfare,
and the band plays louder every day.

Every summer Anson had a window box of flowers
Near the milk house door
And every morning after chores
he watered them and then
with the thumb and forefinger of his calloused hand
he gently, gently plucked
the dying blossoms.

As I was saying, last May, on a Saturday, Anson and Marie
sold out. It was a good day.
Anson's prayers were answered.
He'd asked God not to let it rain.
As the sun came up Norman Pelletier—
The auctioneer—
drove down Route 15 and up over the hill
to here and told Marie
to have an hour's worth of junk

to get the people started.

By ten o'clock trucks lined both sides of the road
Either way from their house half a mile to ours
And that far the other way too.
It was a farmer's auction, too early in the year
for summer people hunting antiques.
There weren't any antiques anyway.
Marie moved around the crowd forcing a smile and waving
like a maitre d' serving up her life.

There was soda and hot dogs
and kids running around screaming, excited by the crowd.
Edith cried. So did Marie. Anson wanted to but didn't.
The farmers stood around and bid, raising a hand quietly
nodding a head,
but there weren't any jokes.
They knew they were playing bit parts in a movie
about their own deaths.

At the end of the day
Anson had taken in thirty-seven thousand dollars
and all that in just machinery and stock.
Everybody said he done real good, *real* good.
But it wasn't good enough.

Anson's working as a mechanic in Burlington now.
He makes a hundred ten dollars a week for his family of four.
They've got a trailer in a trailer park.
We saw them a couple of months ago.
They said they missed it up here on the hill.

Farmwork　　　　　　　　　　　**Lenard D. Moore**

April sunlight, the distant
field filled with dust;
black men in black boots
hoist fertilizer
while others pull tobacco plants
up from the warm earth.

Beneath a near pine
three women wait, quiet
among old stones
while I stand by,
having planted tobacco,
listening to a hidden bird's song.

Working Class　　　　　　　　　**Lenard D. Moore**

(for Angela Jackson)

The blues dig rows
in sun-hot
fields.
A girl hands her daddy's
history to the woman
looping tobacco.
A boy slaps his mama's
clues of tobacco blues
beneath his arms
as his footprints
crush yards of hurt.
A man clenches his fist
and walks and walks
round in his troubles,
swallowing words
in his throat,
digesting
vowels of Motherland's
culture.
A woman recites

what her mother's
mother told of whips
cracking and
snapping strong backs.
Blues
haunt wherever they slow-walk
down
long rows sprinkled
and sprinkled
with dusty tears.

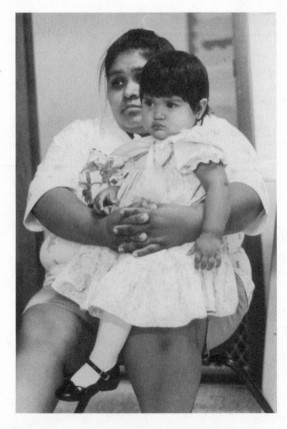

Migrant Head Start Program, Ohio © Becky Dickerson

From the Field   Lenard D. Moore

Certainly they are the same weathered trees
we carved our names on,
played on as children, making
an insistent sound. Two elms rub together
and bend. Out here, no one listens.
They go on pulling tobacco plants
from the damp black earth.
Some load plants on flatbeds
on the puddle side roads.
Only a young girl stands
at the end of a row
not working.
Twenty years ago,
we pulled plants
at any age. Children
won't do field work anymore.
Who is content on bent knees,
except when praying? I would kneel
to uproot plants
in warm daylight.
But I stand dreaming
about my people's labored hands.
The thick clouds do not move.
The day goes on this way
until sun leaves
like yesterday
into the deepest stillness
of tobacco country.
Rich soil linked us
like blessings that speak to us
without a sound.

On Factory Avenue   Thom Tamarro

When we reach the stop sign near his old mill on Factory Avenue, my
father glances toward the gatehouse and, as if on cue, begins telling me
how he loved filing through those gates when the 3 o'clock whistle blew
and punching his time card. In the parking lot you'd hear guys happy to
be done with work, he tells me, guys yelling at each other and doors
slamming and engines starting and dirt and gravel flying all over the place.
He points toward old man Cioffi's place and tells me how he'd head
toward George's Market on 12th Street, sometimes stopping off at the
European Bakery on 11th and buying a fresh loaf of Vienna bread for
supper. As I pull away from the stop sign, he's mapping out all of this to
me with the sweep of his arm, hand and finger, carving an invisible route
in the air because the mill's been closed for nearly twenty years, the gate
house and parking lot empty, there's no more European Bakery or
George's Market, and strangers live in Cioffi's place. It's as though he's
still back there, listening to something far off and long ago, conducting the
music of his life on Factory Avenue.

I hear longing in his voice as it trails off to the present. It's the real world
symphony, the 3 o'clock steam whistle howling at him as he turns away
from all that and asks me if I remember the night—a few months after
the mill shut down and he lost his job after thirty-one years—I found him
collapsed on the bathroom floor, his stomach ruptured in ulcers. He asks
me if I remember. And I do.

We turn off Factory Avenue onto the highway and head for the airport so
I can catch a plane for home. He's listening to a music only he can hear.
Something none of us can imagine. How easily life is diminished. How
difficult it must be to turn away from the beautiful music of America.

Lions After Slumber   Dane Cervine

Poetry used to be worth the world, before cloistered
in academic circles, resplendent in literary silk, dead.

But in 1909, women of the Ladies Garment Union
pressed on against winter, scabs, prison
reciting *Mask of Anarchy* as they worked inside the
Triangle Shirtwaist Company in New York City:

> *Rise like lions after slumber, shake your chains*
> *to earth...Ye are many, they are few!*

When fire broke out in the rag bin, sweeping through
illegal floors with locked doors too high for the ladders
to reach, the New York *World* responded in lyric:

> *They jumped with their clothing ablaze...*
> *they leapt with their arms around each other,*
> *onto growing piles of the dead and dying.*

When it was over, one hundred thousand marched
down Broadway, because it mattered,
because the twenty seven thousand killed on the job
every year at the turn of this great century
made silent poems of their lives, because Joe Hill
was charged with murder as he sang, lyrics inciting
the downtrodden to throw off their chains
as gospel hymns the slaves before—

and because his poetry mattered, he was executed
by firing squad in Utah, calling man, woman and child,
black and white, immigrants all, to do something
tangible, now.

Which Langston Hughes did in the 30's,
wedding the poem to the world rather than the classroom,
calling to the people

> *Who made America,*
> *Whose sweat and blood, whose faith and pain...*
> *Must bring back our mighty dream again...America!*

Poetry must rise as a lion after slumber,
hunt game of import, roar with every stroke,
for we cannot matter to the world
if the world does not matter to us.

© Photo by Jim Lang

Part Four

Life on the Streets

Life on the Streets

A.D. Winans

it's an all night horror show
hookers pimps transvestites
on the go

it's hollywood glitter
a night at the ritz
it's bath houses and porno flicks
it's lonely vaginas in search of dicks

it's keystone cops and neon lights
it's gaudy women in tights
it's the phantom of the opera
in a grotesque mask

it's a wino donor
it's an old man with a boner
it's CBS reporting the evening news
it's john lee hooker singing the blues

it's one too many church bells
it's poor folks going through hell
it's pilgrims on the way to the shrine
it's police informers dropping a dime
it's politicians wallowing in slime

it's a miracle… it's a crime
it's a million windshield wipers
it's a billion disposable diapers

It's a rainbow with fading hues
it's children with no shoes
it's hank williams singing:
STOP THE WORLD I WANT TO GET OFF
It's doctors practicing the
hypocritical oath

it's sport cars and caviar
it's a dying man puking out his guts
at the corner bar
it's al capone doing time on the rock

it's a miracle in the womb
it's the dead and dying
living in a tomb

it's a waiter in a bow tie
it's the pope selling the big lie
it's a woman giving birth
it's corporate america picking
the bones of the dead

it's the slave masters
with shackles and chains
it's bill gates and glittering dames
it's garment workers toiling

in sweat shops
it's pickled pork feet and chops
it's corrupt politicians and cops
it's the death of the beats
it's life on the streets

Ladybug, Ladybug

Victoria Rivas

Mitzi was our neighborhood hooker.
I babysat her kids. Four of them,
from three years old to eight. They were close.

They didn't talk much. Mitzi left them
alone when she couldn't pay me. One
night they lit matches. I heard fire trucks

from miles away. The house and kids were
black and dead. One fire fighter tried to
give the baby mouth to mouth, but the

limp child's lips came off on his. Those kids
would most likely have grown up to be
factory workers, maybe their wives.

Maybe not. I wonder if Mitzi
is still alive. I wonder if she   [Missing text]

On Telegraph Avenue   Jonathan Hayes

She sits cross-legged, in the sun, with sweet chili lips,
sandalwood skin and eyes, eyes of the moon.

Her long black hair drops down. Kissing her dog,
her lips in fur, she smells the funk, the pure truth of all living things.

She looks up and says,

"Spare change?"

Good Afternoon   Jonathan Hayes

he placed a deaf card
on the tacqueria table
it said, "will you buy me? any price accepted"

as he retrieved his cards from the other tables
and made his way back to me
i lifted a plastic basket that held tortilla chips
and offered them to him

he opened his mouth wide
and pointed that he had no teeth

Radar   Dane Cervine

There was a man
unraveling down the sidewalk along
    the backside of the Capitol's Rotunda
  a man vexed
  all in a wrangle
  arm through a tattered vet jacket
 holding a black phone receiver
 talking loud trying to get through
 to somebody...
    but it was an old 50's phone
frayed cord dangling from the mouthpiece—
      it wasn't connected
    and no-one was listening.

There was a woman
whimsical and wiry as a homeless gypsy
    worn red jacket and yellow scarves
    radiating so bright
    she'd be impossible to miss
unless that was your plan
      smiled as I passed
    caught that glint in my eye like
    a hidden wavelength
      called out behind me
How are you today? Yes you, you look alive!
  and I am and wonder
    how she knows...
    an invisible beam
   emanating between agents
   secret in the wrong country.

There were three cadets
young white and true blue jogging by
     in grey shorts neatly cut hair
    innocent and clean as the sons
    you're supposed to have
   chuckling between easy breaths
   eyes like radar
  scanning for what is out of place

on their tracking screens
                    light on we other three
          circling the capitol looking
                         for a way in
               and I
          wondering will we show up
                         as friend or foe.

Solstice

David Mason

Just off the Interstate, a red-haired man
stands in near-zero cold, holding a sign.
Need money for bus, it says. *God bless you.*
A man all dirt and beard and ruddiness,
stomping his unlaced boots to warm himself.
I lower my window, hand him two singles
and ask him where he's headed. *Amarillo.*
I got a wife and two kids waiting for me.

Maybe it's true. Beyond the overpass
a liquor store's red sign winks on and off,
and there's a bar a little further down.
Wishing him luck, I take my own road home.
The uphill flow of traffic after work
speeds and slows in one obedient pack,
some of us singing, or listening to the news
in early dark, December's shortest day.

Soon Orion will rise above my house
and I will pause before stepping inside,
as if the stars and I could intercede
somewhere beyond this theatre of doubt—
how I half-heard a stranger's hard-luck story,
assuming he was one who'd end up drunk,
booted out at closing time to mumble
Amarillo. God bless. Got to get back home.

crossroads   **Christopher Cunningham**

between
two busy city streets
there is a
gas station store
and out front
and to one side
stands a bum
in dirty grey pants
and sweat ringed t-shirt.

his hair is greasy and plastered
to his skull from the
southern humidity.
he cocks his head to one side,
and picks his teeth
with an extended pinkie finger.
he eyes the people
getting gas,
washing car windshields,
coming from the store.
he sizes up the handouts.

the sun sets behind the store,
the sweat on his face visible
in the red lights and
onrushing dusk.

money is invigorating:
when you have it,
you are somebody.
when you don't,
you can only afford
to
be
yourself,

hands
out,
waiting.

he checks his finger
then moves toward the guy
pumping gold card gallons into his
Lexus.

everyone
is
someone else's
mark.

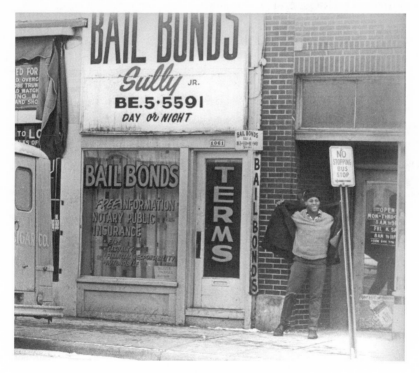

© Photo by Jim Lang

Dan   **A.D. Winans**

He has crow's feet eyes
and weather beaten skin
walks with a limp
and a stooped back
He lives in an old trailer
with his dog
Bones
who is just that
Sleeps under newspaper
thin blankets
prowls trash cans
for other people's leftovers
too proud to seek General Assistance

He warms his food
on an illegal gas burner
his body with cheap wine
when his morning rounds
of picking up recyclable cans
pays him enough
His door is always open
His hand never out
His produce crate night stand
filled with Whitman, Pound
Keats and Shelley

And the World Sparkled like Glittered Paper   Steven Skovensky

Cynthia and I were walking down Irving Park Road. A late September evening in Chicago, Illinois. I stopped and looked down near my feet—a shiny quarter lay in my path, right where I was walking, with Cynthia. She stopped when she no longer heard my footsteps marching alongside hers. What? She asked. A quarter, I motioned, there's a quarter on the ground. It's an evening in September, Chicago, late September, as we pass a bevy of closed businesses and restaurants. Some closed until Monday, some only until the sun, that giant ball of fire, seizes a Sunday morning sky. It still has a while left to burn. Everyone on this planet gets a little heat. Not everybody gets a home.

We had just gotten off the el, coming from a shoe warehouse where I bought a pair of size fifteen clearance shoes for seventeen dollars. That was where we were coming from when I found the quarter. The shoes were only seventeen dollars. I sound like my Great Uncle Melvin when I talk like that. He always knew how much money he had in his pockets, the bank he churned through his old, cracked fingers. Uncle Melvin died last year. He was a veteran of what they called the Last Great War. He met and married my Aunt Elsa in Germany. She had been married to one of Hitler's Secret Service officers. She was a waitress in Nazi Germany and once saw Hitler come through tight-lined parade streets. My Aunt Elsa hated bagels because of who made them, what went along with that, but that's another story, another whole thing in itself. I want to get back to Cynthia and I finding that quarter on Irving Park Road, what we said about that.

About Uncle Melvin, though, and about the Great War: he told his friend, Dos Paul, in Belsano, Pennsylvania, that he didn't think that the Army would take him. *I got bad teeth*, he said. *Hell Melvin*, Dos Paul said to him, *they want you to kill the Germans, not eat 'em*. Uncle Melvin used to pay me two dollars to wash and wax his car. He lived through the Depression. He liked to wear his fifty-cent K-Mart hat and tell people how much it had cost him. *Fifty-cents,* he said, flicking the brim. There's a picture of us, taken when I was ten or eleven, standing by his old gray automobile. He was visiting us in Ohio. Uncle Melvin is wearing a white dress shirt, sprigs of white hair showing at the top of his chest, drinking coffee from a tiny mug, wearing a calm and proud smile. I'm wearing red, white and blue, green A-Team hat and blue pants. My eyes are closed and I'm growing into my long arms, the ones hanging down to my knees. But Uncle Melvin is smiling and I'm proud of that picture.

Cynthia and I were walking down Irving Park Road and I found a quarter. It was a cool Chicago evening, late September and we were walking towards her house, thinking of stopping at Katarina's for a cup of coffee. Katarina is a wonderful Greek woman who runs a coffee shop on Irving Park. On the outside a sign reads, 'Street of Dreams' in Greek. There is a posterboard poem taped to the window that ends with, *Hope More, Fear Less.* Everyone is welcome inside and she allows real people to play real music. There's no games or hocus pocus: if you've got a story to tell, the microphone is on and the coffee is brewing. Katarina said that Cynthia means 'Moon Goddess' in Greek. I have also seen it as 'Goddess of Wild Animals.' Growing up in the Methodist Church, I was always reminded that Steven was stoned to death in the Bible. Everybody's name means something. Everything dropped and found has a story. It means something. A place like Katarina's allows a story to unfold. Katarina's, in Chicago.

About the quarter: I found it on the edge of a crack, on the sidewalk we were walking on. I told Cynthia my dad raised us to look down when we walk, to prowl the concrete and corners of the grass for money. She asked why. I fumbled on my words for a minute, like fingertips feeling for a nickel in a pocket of change. Then, *Because that's what my dad's like. That's kind of the way we were raised. We weren't poor but we didn't have luxuries that some families had.* He trained my brother and I to scour the ground for extras, bumpers to our pockets, rewarded in our finds with money for comic books, candy bars and professional wrestling magazines. When my dad hit big at the track, he would stop at Dairy Mart and buy me a copy of Professional Wrestling Illustrated and forty-four ounces of Mountain Dew. I would drink pop until my stomach hurt. I read about and believed in the heroism of Jerry 'The King' Lawler, 'Rowdy' Roddy Piper and Hulk Hogan. My dad worked two jobs when his family was young; my mom stayed home to raise us in their image. When *Star Wars* came out, my dad took my brother to see it; my mom played games with me at home. Maybe we played Candy Land. I was afraid to go. All of this has to do with me finding the quarter on Irving Park Road. In Chicago. With Cynthia. It all has to do with how I got from Ohio to here.

I'm still trying to tell Cynthia about why I was raised to look for money, when I walked around, as a kid. It's not that I was raised to avoid looking at people or things, though I know my parents worried about the gaze of strangers and strange people. They worried that I would walk off with someone else, at a flea market or store, if I wasn't paying attention. That never happened. I guess I was raised to observe the world, not just the people in it. Raised to appreciate simple joy in finding a quarter, even a dollar on the ground. Since then, I've translated that joy into something else: finding a discarded grocery list, a letter in a dumpster, a Target sales ad with handwriting in the margins. Finding these things, absolutely true, and telling a story about them. How the grocery list asking for bread, eggs, beans, bananas and suppositories tells about the struggle of the small family, crunching numbers at the table, crunching cereal in the kitchen, surviving the long march of snowy hunger. I've tried to write stories about found objects and now I'm trying to write this, about talking to Cynthia on Irving Park Road, sun moving onto somewhere else, Noon Hour Grill across the street, closed for dinner, pancake batter in the refrigerator turning into Jell-O.

My dad used to conduct training exercises to hone our skill in searching for bounty. At the park or at Sea World, he would shoot ahead of us, an advance scout prepping the path, preparing our drills. He would drop dollar bills on the ground and meander back to our tiny footsteps. We'd walk past the planted money, the potted finds, to continue our pursuit. He'd pick up the money and show us what we had missed. He never told us that it was his money, he had put it there, that really he was no better off than the minute before. I believed then that money was abundant in the world, you just had to look for it. If I didn't believe in money trees than I believed in an occasional dollar popping forth as a mushroom. That there were tiny hives of dollars, quarters grew out of cracks, pennies obvious as stones. The idea of money being hard to make and keep was unknown to me. I didn't know how hard it was for my dad, how hard he worked. He was an overnight guard at Sea World in Aurora the first summer it was open. During the day he worked at a plastics factory.

My Uncle Melvin and Aunt Elsa had an apple tree in their front yard when they lived in Pennsylvania. My cousin, unemployed and on welfare, lived down the road from them. Uncle Melvin invited him to come take all the apples in his yard, the ones that had fallen from the tree. My cousin didn't come. Uncle Melvin could never understand how a guy who didn't have a job wouldn't come over and pick up all the free apples he wanted, out of his own uncle's yard. My cousin still had some dirt floors in his house and a blind mother who lived in his living room. Cats slept in the oven. While I'm thinking about it, there's something that happened years ago, at the Aurora flea market, when I was a kid, walking with my dad. It's not about free apples, my uncle, cousin or blind aunt. I was a kid, walking with my dad. He was smoking a cigarette. I reached up to hold his hand. My little palm buried into the hot cherry of his smoke. My whole body recoiled and howled like a carnival barker, stirring dusty and expired toys on all the tables. My dad put out his smoke and wiped my hand, maybe kissed it and hugged me like a soldier heading off to fight the Great War. I had never seen him sorrier for anything in his life, or mine.

I told Cynthia a little about why I look for money when I walk, but I didn't tell her all these stories. Before I forget, here's another one, one of my favorites: Uncle Melvin and Aunt Elsa eventually moved from the house with the apple tree in the front yard. They had an auction. My Uncle Tink was in town with his wife, Aunt Corky. Aunt Corky was my mom's sister. Uncle Tink, with his rough, loveable façade, went into Elsa's kitchen to see what was for lunch. Now Uncle Tink was a sailor, lived on a sub for years, had forgotten social graces that keep a society from strangling itself. He looked at a dish on her table, a relish salad meticulously garnered with green sprigs and ivy and twigs. Before Aunt Elsa could say what it was, Uncle Tink put his pointer finger in his mouth and gagged. Like a schoolboy he groaned, *Looks like somebody threw up.* He smiled and was never offered so much as a cup of coffee in her house again. Uncle Tink was only speaking his language, crude as an oil slick, but honest.

There is a lot of money to be found in Chicago, even outside of September, loose change sitting in cracks or sleeping on the streets. There are a lot of stories in Chicago, people sleeping in bars, heads full of stories, people sleeping in streets or shelters, shelter blankets wrapped around countless men. They all have stories and know the value of a dollar. I know men in Chicago who are smart enough to believe they'll find more broken bottles than dollar bill mushrooms. A cup of shelter coffee is bitter tonic and the truth of a life sets in when the sun comes up, unconcerned if you don't have a place of your own.

This summer I saw a wild man scouring the corners of Grant Park, scanning the ground with a metal detector. He wore a chain around his neck that held every piece of metal he had ever found-rings, earrings, bracelets, bottle openers, lucky charms, washers and odd bits of metal, necklace holes drilled in the middle. He looked like a skinny, white Mr. T. When his buzzer went off he plunged to the ground and maniacally hacked into the soft earth with a steak knife. Again, I thought of my father, who bought a new maroon metal detector at Sears one summer. After finding all the change we had ever lost in our yard, the neighbor's wedding ring and Coca Cola bottles two feet into the earth, we began going to area playgrounds, parks and deserted landscapes. He made six hundred dollars by investing a hundred and fifty on that simple device. He found money, rare coins, rings, dogtags and junk with no business being made of metal. When it was all over he sold it to Joey across the street for ten bucks. Before Joey bought it, the metal detector stretched across a card table at my dad's garage sale. It said something, about where things had been.

My dad and I would go to Campus Elementary School, about a mile from our house, to play on the monkey bars and pillage the ground for valuables. I would climb to the top of the slide and declare it something else. The tower of a great ship, a Navy vessel or whaling ship, the highest point of an Army base. Far off in the field I could see my dad, swinging that metal detector back and forth, constant hum and occasional buzz when he found somebody's lunch money. I knew he was looking for that, or maybe a ring lost from the hand's of an older boy. He had few other expectations. But I pretended something else. From my Army fort I saw my dad hunting for landmines, searching for traps that could turn parts of me into worthless kites. My dad, an ex-Marine, was making the world safer for my friends and me. Soldier of fortune or of good fortune, he must have still looked like a madman.

My Uncle Melvin was given a military funeral in a tiny cemetery in Belsano. He was buried near his sister, my grandmother. After the funeral and drive to the plot, all of his buddies from the local VFW post arrived to begin their precious ritual. One read from a book while the rest fired guns into the air. As these proud men strode past us, up the hill, guns at their sides, my dad looked at me. Their steps were slow and their walk was tepid. This was before they fired the guns. Those men who had seen the Big One, WWII, had certain sadness in their march, done too many times. They looked at the ground. *Oh jeez,* my dad whispered, *they've got guns. Hope they haven't been at the bar all morning.* After the playing of Taps and pronouncement of blanks into the cold Keystone air, they folded up the American Flag and presented it to my aunt. She may have moved into a nursing home with bagels on the menu.

While I'm thinking of it, listen to this-it's about Uncle Melvin. He knew the value of a dollar. Before he died, he occupied his favorite barstool at the Twin Rocks Tavern, a smoky hole filled with men who had war stories, men who worked in the mines, men with broken hearts, broken homes. The Twin Rocks Tavern sold beer for a quarter a cup-until a State Liquor Agent came in and busted up the show. Maybe he had four cups for a dollar, wiped his mustache and wrote them a ticket, I don't know. The tavern was fined five thousand dollars. Uncle Melvin smiled when he told me that, the next week, they started charging fifty cents a cup to pay off the fine. He smiled big when he told me that.

Back here in Chicago, where I live now, I'm still looking for money. Maybe now more than ever. I'm digging up stories. That's how I've arrived to all this. When I first moved here, I worked all-night in a men's shelter. The sound of 65 men sleeping on shelter beds is wind knocked out of a stomach. They're not really beds, anyway. They are little plastic mats. They are little plastic forests of blue germs. Lice and fleas sleep in the folds of clothing but Jerry's snore blows away any bedbug not shuttered in. The shelter serves peanut butter and jelly day-old bagel sandwiches. Some of the guys don't have teeth to chew with. Marcus, Indian Warrior who sleeps in bed #50, has teeth and will sell you them or a poem for meal money. Anyway, I'm still working with men who have broken hearts, holes in their pockets and scars running the length of their frames. Each scar has a story. If you buy a fellow enough Old Crow, you might hear all of them. They'll tell you about their great war. They don't need metal detectors to find blade marks on them. Get them drunk and they won't try to hustle you. Find Tom at the Wooden Nickel and he'll fill you up with heart, stories, and Wild Turkey. Most of the men I know give thanks year round, thankful for even what they don't have. If they do find a money tree, they cut it down and spend to the stump. They all had a childhood once, some kind of family. They're aching to hold hands with their daddies tonight.

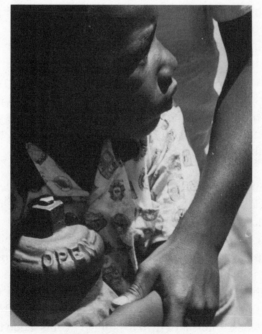

© Photo by Jim Lang

Exhibit After the Poetry Reading   **Cherelyn Willet**

In this room I escape
the loud clatter of socializing.
The track lighting buzzes overhead.
A white room so large
it could sleep twelve comfortably,
but only disembodied red
oil legs on canvas live here.

Naked jaundiced women
with lop-sided breasts
dive into coffins,
while a burgundy couple
makes love
in front of a pile of burning corpses.
Someone paid good money
to put a plaque next to that crap
with their name on it.

I think about the faces
a block away,
the dancing sounds of their language,
the smell of their greenish noodle soup
cooked in the open air,
and what they wouldn't give to have a room like this
and a pillow to sleep on.

Welfare   Cherelyn Willet

Our distant faces
are numbers
to them behind
the bullet proof windows.
They take our papers
and shoo us away.
They give us monopoly money
and not a single smile
or prayer
or even acknowledgement
that we are people.
We thought we were better once too.

Cannery   Jonathan Hayes

sat on the dock
all night, listening
to the water whisper
a sea shanty

tomorrow
the boats will be back
full of salmon

and workers on the line
standing next to loud machines
will sing during twelve-hour shifts

without opening their mouths

Part Four

Diabled List

© Photo by Jim Lang

Union Meeting, 1959 **Thom Tamarro**

Once during the dark winter of 1959,
I walked with my father to a
union meeting at the AFL-CIO Hall,
where inside rumors of walkouts and strike
gathered us, and men offered
cigarettes without the asking.

When Bruno Nardelli called the meeting to order,
he said he just returned from Pittsburgh where
the owners were still unwilling to meet with him.
Then Bruno opened the floor for discussion.
Mario Tomasi said although he had twelve children,
a wife, and a mother and father living under the same roof,
he would be the first to walk and lead his men
from Plant 6 to the picket lines.
And Stavros Petrakis yelled, "Ya, me too!"
Then Marcello Rugetti stood up and shouted,
"Let the bastards carry slag to their own heaps,"
to the thundering claps of the workers.

Walking home, we passed the gates and fences
of U.S. Steel, moved toward the blast furnaces
whose burning orange lit all our lives,
the furnaces that burn year round
except for two weeks in the summer
when the whole plant shuts down,
and the lucky men get to crawl inside
to scrape them clean.
Closer, we felt flames, warm on our faces,
so we took off our coats and walked the rest
of the way home in sweatshirts and sweaters.

Beyond these fences, nothing else mattered.
The whole world was here. Later, we felt
sleet turn to snow as we made our way
along the dim streets above the frozen river,
catching glimpses of ourselves in store windows,
watching our shadows go before us
into that long night, those fires burning deep
and bright into the center of our lives.

The Clearances   David Mason

In memory of the dead at Ludlow, Colorado, April 1914

Below the mountain, talus,
below the talus, slag,
below the slag the mineshaft
and the empty moneybag.

My stubborn Scottish forebears
fled sorrow on a dare.
America was uncleared land.
They staked out their share.

One settled in Missouri,
one fought in Tennessee.
One rode to Colorado
with a cook from Italy.

He built by coal-seamed foothills
a clapboard mercantile,
selling flour for miners' scrip
in dusty Cedar Hill.

When miners struck at Ludlow,
machine guns raked the tents.
Old folksongs still remember
the slaughter of innocents,

but it wasn't the flames or gunfire,
it was the price of steel
that closed the mine at Ludlow
and the town of Cedar Hill.

Now try to find their houses
or any blessed trace
left from the desert clearances
where wind blows through the grass.

The sunbleached skin of a doll
and broken bottle's glare

are all you will find among
clumps of prickly pear.

Below the mountain, talus,
below the talus, slag,
below the slag the mineshaft
and the empty moneybag.

The "Outhouse"   **Sandra Lee Stillwell**

On summer days
tourists would stop
to tell us that our "outhouse"
was on fire.

The "Old Man" would smile
and explain,
while he sat on his bucket
mending the nets he sold and rented,
that, "Oh no," we had indoor plumbing.

It was only the smokehouse,
where he smoked his fish
and then he would sell some fish
to those tourists
the money warm in his pockets.

The following summer,
they would find their way back
to the little house
where the "Old Man"
sat on his bucket
smoking Pall Mall's
and mending nets.

While, there in the background
the smokehouse
gently puffed out smoke below its eaves
scenting the neighborhood
with the sweet smell of alder wood
and brown sugar.

Disabled List   **Will Watson**

Ever the smart ass, Red Husiar sports
a polaroid of his stump pumping blood.
The recorder shot it right after
he called the meat wagon, while
the rest of us rigged a tourniquet
from a wrench and some rags
and tried not to act as sick as we felt.
Now, Red leans into a bear fat cloud
and pours heavy gauge through number two.
Ask about the hook, and he cracks
"It played hell with my piano lessons,
 but you get used to just about anything"

Sheet wrapping, piece work, four-eyes Terry D.
honed his buck knife so sharp
he could trim three two-ply crates in one
swipe which could really add up on payday
but he never figured he'd slip and slash
his finger tendons instead of cardboard
and they took our knives away
the only tools we owned ourselves.
Funny thing, it hardly left a scar
though the hand looked like a claw.
Cold days Terry'd tuck it into his crotch
to get the blood flowing.

Henry Ciezahn found five tons
would drive a steel toe boot
clean through his foot
and weld the whole mess to the floor
licketysplit. When Human Resources got him
this really nifty boot and brace
for where his toes used to be
Troy, our crazy redneck roller,
took to calling him Gunsmoke.
He'd yell "Mister Dillon! Mister Dillon!"
when Henry'd clomp down the catwalk
but the crew figured even a mean joke
was better than acting like nothing
had happened. What do you think?

Worst I ever saw though
was Hi Highlands cut in two
by a seven-foot twenty-ton batch anneal
just hot enough to cauterize
everything it didn't squash.
So he didn't bleed to death
or go off the deep end and still works
the pickle forty a week summer winter
midnights, days, four-to-twelves
like everybody else, pretty much,
always bullshitting about "my better half"
his big, veiny left arm
enough to make a weightlifter wince.
That's real class, if you ask me.

© Photo by Jim Lang

Graveyard Shift

John Thompson

Joey was running late, but he stopped anyway when Scully offered him a smoke. He tried not to stare as Scully used the stub of his
right arm to flip open his chrome lighter. Most of the arm had been lost in
the corrugator years earlier. The joke around the plant was that since
Scully had given so much to the company, International Paper had found a
job he could do with one hand tied behind his back. He moved material,
using a specially equipped forklift. Scully dressed specially, too, in white
button down dress shirts, always short-sleeved, even in winter. Joey had
known one other one-armed person in grade school, and if Celeste caught
you looking, she'd pick her nose and put the snot on her stub and eat it.

"McCoy!" Joey turned to see the foreman, Drysdale, the only
boss around on third shift, looking at his pocket watch. Its gold chain
dangled from his massive hand. Everything about Drysdale was big, his
neck, his head, his torso- but a critic had recently scribbled DRYSDALE'S
A NEEDLE DICK on the men's room wall. "We start at 11:00, not five
after," he said, snapping his watch shut. "I had to replace you on the
printer." Joey knew what came next. "You're on the corrugator." Drysdale
crossed his Popeye forearms, ready for an argument, but Joey just shrugged.
There was no point arguing. He'd fucked up; he'd stalled coming to work,
avoiding the inevitable until he had to drive like a maniac and still be five
minutes late.

"Hop on," yelled Scully as Drysdale walked away.

Joey sat on wooden pallets being carried on the forks and took a
slow drag off his cigarette. Smoking, like riding on the forklift, could only
be done on the graveyard shift when there were no suits around. He rode
past industrial gray and green machinery, everything uniform and replace-
able and loud, all the way across the plant to the corrugator where William
was already working. William wore his trademark chartreuse bandanna,
and his work boots were laced with matching glow-in-the-dark tassels, a
throwback to his days as a middleweight contender.

William grabbed a bundle of cardboard, squared it with his open
hand, then hoisted it, turned and slammed it shoulder high on the wooden
pallet to his left. He immediately spun back to the steel chute for the next
one. His skin was already sweat-soaked, a rich mahogany; the glowing
headband and laces highlighted its deep purple hue. His body looked the
same as when he fought, though now his muscles were sculpted from
years on the corrugator, a dinosaur of moving parts a city block long that
ingested elephant sized rolls of brown paper, three at a time, at one end,
and shit cardboard bundles out the other. Each new man, as a rite of

passage, started out on the corrugator before graduating to a less brutal job.

Scully stopped the forklift beside William and yelled, "I got something for ya, William." Joey snuffed his cigarette on the floor. The sweat from William's brow stained the top board as he smacked a bundle onto the stack. Joey tied his own bandanna on, gypsy style. William turned to grab the next bundle, which had already begun to roll down the chute. "You ready?" he yelled.

Joey nodded as he moved in behind William who hoisted another bundle, turned, stacked it, and moved out of the way. Joey stepped in and, keeping with the rhythm, snagged the next bundle as it careened down the steel rollers. The razor edge of a cardboard sheet sliced into his palm. He cursed, then lifted, turned and stacked the bundle before he sucked the deep paper cut below his thumb, knowing from experience it wouldn't be the last of the night. Gloves didn't work, tearing to shreds in a matter of minutes. Band-Aids sweated off. The only protection was not to let a sharp edge get a slicing angle. It came with practice, and Joey, who hadn't been stuck on the corrugator for months, was out of practice. Before he could worry about the cut, the next bundle was there. He grabbed it and repeated the motions he'd make three to four times a minute for the next seven and three-quarter hours.

"I'm gonna crank `er up now," William yelled. "You okay till I get back?"

Joey nodded. Without the needed men, William would not only run the corrugator, but he'd unload with Joey, too. The control panel was a half block away. Joey knew he'd be okay until William got to the controls. Then he'd have to keep up until William sprinted back, or they'd have a hell of a mess.

Joey intended to keep up, and he did, barely. By the time William got back, Joey's right palm was bleeding onto the cardboard. His left hand stung, though not as bad as the right. William stepped in beside him to take every other bundle, and things calmed to a steady grab, straighten, lift, turn, stack, get ready to grab again. William even managed to light a cigarette, throwing the spent match at the No Smoking sign above his head before needing to catch the next bundle. The only diversion from the droning sameness until 1:00 AM was the periodic arrival and departure of Scully to drop off more pallets and to take away the fully stacked ones. Drysdale came by, too, though they didn't actually see him at the far end of the corrugator, but the increased pitch told them he'd been at the controls, cranking it up a bit, and the bundles would be coming faster now. "Prick." William spat on the next bundle. "He knows I'm short two men."

Scully rolled up just as the last bundle before break rolled down the chute. Joey and William ignored it. The three of them went out on the fire exit landing and sat on milk crates. The landing beat walking to the cafeteria at the other end of the plant where most of the men met, since it would have been time to turn around and walk back again by the time Joey and William got there. Besides, the landing had fresh air, a relief even in winter, and an expansive sky with a universe filled with possibilities removed from the plant. They all peed off the landing, their urine pounding the asphalt twenty feet below. William and Joey would have smoked a joint if Scully hadn't joined them. He wouldn't rat on them, but it wasn't worth freaking him out. They smoked their cigarettes and rested. Joey wanted some water before they started up again, and the fountain was close by so he went in early. He drank greedily and then ran cold clean water over his raw hands. He blew on them to stop the burning, but it didn't work. The bell sounded at 1:10 AM. Scully climbed aboard his lift as Drysdale approached. One by one machines began to growl throughout the plant.

"I'll start it up," said Drysdale, signaling William to stay back with Joey. Behind Drysdale's back Scully hunched over so his stump reached his crotch and massaged his dick before roaring off in the other direction.

"No love lost there," said Joey.

"You got that right." William adjusted his headband. The corrugator began to pound. William's lips moved again. Joey wanted to hear more about Scully and Drysdale but the plant's roar was deafening. A bundle rolled down the chute and he snatched it. William got the next one, and so it went on without let up until lunch at 3:00 AM.

Scully zoomed up with a fresh pallet just as the lunch bell rang. "Hop on," he yelled.

"Not me," said William holding up the bag his wife had packed. He handed Joey a sweat soaked dollar. "Get me a Pepsi, okay?"

"Okay," said Joey as he climbed onto the forklift for a ride to the lunchroom.

"Hold on tight," said Scully as he lit a cigarette. Then he tore off.

Joey was already loading quarters into the candy machine when others began to shuffle in. Two operators sat at a table, both with the bloodshot, half-high daze of four hours of inhaled ink fumes. The taller one still had a clean stripe around his midsection where his rubber apron had been. The rest of him was speckled with blue ink blotches, but his polished Harley Davidson belt buckle sparkled at the peak of his beer gut. Ink dotted the other printer's green work clothes and his forearms so that it was hard to tell where the prison tattoos ended and tonight's ink began. A magazine was rolled into the slot of his lunch pail where the thermos belonged. He spread the magazine on the table. "How'd ya like to slap your dick against this babies?" he said to Joey as he pointed to a picture of a busty woman who cupped her breasts under an erect penis. Splotches of semen dripped from her cheeks, her eyes were blank. "I'm not so sure she's enjoying her work," said Joey moving to the next vending machine with sodas.

"Who the fuck cares?" the printer said pulling the magazine back.

Joey shrugged and bent for his cola.

Marty came in and sat at another table by himself. His hair and his short beard were neatly trimmed. He wore a green work shirt and matching pants, a thick black belt with dangling keys and a folded red bandanna stuck in his back pocket. He opened his lunch pail, then his *Bulletin*, put the paper aside and settled on *Flower and Garden Magazine*. Talk was that Marty raised African violets. Joey nodded and Marty nodded back. Joey had been his helper for a few nights, but Marty hadn't said more than two words. One night Marty had been engrossed in something secretive at his work station, and when Joey had a chance, he sneaked up and looked under the work orders to find a small unlined note pad. Joey knew he shouldn't violate what was private, but looked anyway and found small pencil portraits—Drysdale looking at his watch, Scully in his button-down collar, William adjusting his bandanna and finally one of Joey himself, no watch, no bandana, no fancy shirt, nothing stood out except his lost, haunted eyes. The portrait made him shiver. He placed the notebook back in its hiding place before Marty returned from the men's room and never said a word.

While heading back to the landing, Joey spotted Drysdale alone in the vacant office where he always ate. He always ate by himself.

When Joey joined him out on the landing, William fired up the joint. "Tell me something," said Joey after taking a hit. "How come Scully hates Drysdale?"

"He blames Drysdale for his arm." William sucked on the joint and passed it back.

"No shit."

"Yup. Before he was foreman, Drysdale used to be the operator of the corrugator; Scully was a helper, like you. Board got jammed, so Drysdale told Scully to clear the rollers. Scully figures Drysdale was the operator, not him, and Drysdale should have been up there, not him. Drysdale ought to be the one-armed bandit. I suppose Drysdale should' a shut it down to be safe." William shrugged and took the joint from Joey. "But you don't shut that motherfucker down unless you got to. Scully got careless, put his fingers where they don't belong." William blew marijuana smoke at Joey. "A man's got to be aware of what he's doing at all times."

Joey was getting higher by the second and was glad to see William stub out the joint. "For next break," said William, stuffing the roach into the cellophane of his Marlboro pack.

"How come Scully's working?" asked Joey. "He should be collecting disability or something."

William jumped up. "Could be, if he wanted. He could be getting seventy percent, tax fucking free. Claims he can't get by on that. Shit, it's that watch, man. That's what keeps Scully here."

"Watch?"

William pulled his bandanna off and unrolled it. "The one that used to belong to Scully's old man. The old man got it when he retired from this shit hole, and he gave it to Scully, but the fucking corrugator ate that watch right along with Scully's right arm." William spread his bandanna and brought the corners together. "Ain't that a kick in the ass, McCoy?" He twisted the bandanna, snapped it smartly, and then wrapped it around his head. "When finally you don't have to be nowhere on time, they give you a watch. Cold fucking world." The bandanna squeezed the bottom of his Afro so the top mushroomed out like an atomic cloud. Joey tied his own bandanna back on. It felt like he was gathering his brains back in to a container, but they weren't going back in the way the same way they came out.

William rubbed his lower back and stretched to the right and to the left. "Hell, Scully ought to hate his old man for getting him a job in this shithole, not Drysdale. Drysdale gave him a way out. Seventy fucking percent, tax-free. I'd be out of here in a flash. You know that pocket watch Drysdale's always checking?"

"Sure."

"He got that for Scully after the accident, had it engraved the same as the old man's and everything, except it was a pocket watch." William snickered. "I guess Drysdale figured without an the arm Scully needed a pocket watch."

"Makes sense," said Joey.

"They say Scully threw it at him, right there in the hospital. Couple a hardheaded motherfuckers. Scully comes back, when he could make as much staying at home playing with his self. He wants Drysdale to look at that fucking stub every night. And Drysdale, he's just as wacko. The cocksucker's worn that watch ever since. Pulls it out all the time just to drive Scully crazy."

"Jesus."

"Oh yeah."

The buzzer sounded.

"We got maybe an hour left on this run," said William heading inside." Then we cruise."

They got in place and waited for Drysdale to start the corrugator. Other machinery started to grind. William put his hands together, cracked his fingers and looked at Joey with glazed resolve. "Here we go," he said as the first bundle shot onto the chute.

Maybe it was the marijuana, Joey wasn't sure, but the realization that he could end up at the plant for as long as William hit with the force of an axe handle. Considering this job as temporary was the only way to tolerate it - but he figured none of the men in this place ever thought of this as permanent job when they started. Another bundle of cardboard rolled down the chute, and William grabbed it, flipped it on edge, patted the corner square, and then lifted. A bundle shot at Joey, and he grabbed it. A half an hour later he wasn't sure he could last. His hands had numbed enough that he didn't mind the cuts unless he hit one directly, but his arms were weakening, and his back had begun to tighten. William looked steady, massaged his back and neck between bundles. Joey tried to stay focused so he could grab the bundles without sustaining any more cuts. He didn't think he could stand one more slice.

"Fuck!" William threw a bundle to the floor.

Joey's bundle was cut at an angle. The next one sliding at William was no good, either. Joey threw his to the side as the next came, also askew. He stepped back to look down the corrugator, trying to see what was wrong. Before he could move to check for jams, William pushed him back toward the chute. "I got it," he yelled. "Keep the rollers clear." William ran toward the front of the corrugator, checking the run at various spots as he went. Joey worked to keep up with the avalanche of cardboard, throwing both his and William's board aside. He threw bundles off the back of the machine as fast as he could. After the first few, he didn't even try to keep them on the scrap pallet. He'd clean the mess up later. The important thing was to keep the rollers clear so they could finish this bitch of a run. He saw William, fifty feet away, spring onto the shoulder-high catwalk and disappear. He knew what William was thinking, *just another fifteen fucking minutes and they could call it a night for this order.*

Joey kept checking the board as he tossed it aside. It seemed to be straightening out. William must have gotten the jam cleared. The last few bundles were close to square. Finally, he stacked three on the good pallet. But then the board went fluey, again, worse than before. Joey went to yell to William, but it was no use. There was no way William would hear anything up there. Joey threw more board aside.

It began to pile up around him, but he kept the chutes clear. His hands must have been getting torn up. There was blood all over the box he'd just dropped. He knew he must be cut bad. He reached for the next and saw blood already on it. Before he could pick it up, another bundle slammed into the bloody one with a chartreuse shoelace dangling from between the sheets of cardboard.

Drysdale had tripped the emergency shut off by the time Joey scrambled up onto the catwalk. The corrugator ground slowly to a halt and as it began to quiet, William stopped screaming. He gripped the catwalk above him, and his neck veins looked ready to pop. So did his eyes. His right leg had already been pulled into the rollers and blades up to mid thigh. His left leg was braced against the safety shield so that he was split like a wishbone about to snap. The instant the rollers stopped pulling, William tried to yank his leg free. He pulled against the catwalk. His body flailed, but the leg didn't budge. Joey had seen a raccoon in a leg trap once and its panic was like this. William's eyes widened even more as blood fountained over the safety shield, the brilliant red arching the catwalk. When he stopped flopping, William still gripped the catwalk's rail like it was the secret to life.

Drysdale climbed up on the corrugator. "Mother a God," he moaned. Then he ripped his belt off and wrapped it around William's thigh.

Scully arrived on his forklift.

"Call a fucking ambulance," Drysdale yelled.

Scully went white.

"Go!" Drysdale screamed.

Scully pushed the control lever forward and the fork-lift flew down the aisle.

One by one operators shut down the machinery, the plant quieting in stages, until nothing ran and all the men were gathered at the corrugator. "It's gonna be alright," said Drysdale patting William's shoulder affectionately. "It's gonna be okay." He didn't say it with much conviction but kept on saying it until the paramedics came. They replaced Drysdale's belt with their own tourniquet, and they tried to keep William calm as the maintenance men took enough of the corrugator apart to free him. The other men watched and fidgeted, smoked cigarettes, and said little. Joey climbed down, out of the way of the paramedics and maintenance men, and stood among the others.

"What the fuck happened?" said Marty. Joey had never heard Marty curse and it struck him as obscene. Scully moved closer to listen, but never took his eyes off the corrugator. Joey just shrugged. There was silence, except for the occasional murmur of paramedics and maintenance men up on the corrugator.

William had been trapped for almost an hour by the time the medics called for help to lift him down to the stretcher. Drysdale climbed back up and three other men filled in below the catwalk with Joey. No one said anything, but Joey figured they all needed to see, like he did, how much of William was left. He'd passed out. A plastic splint and bandages covered his right leg and a bloody work boot flopped at the end. He was strapped to the stretcher and a paramedic held a plastic bag that dripped solution into William's arm. They covered all of him with a blanket, except his round black face, chartreuse bandanna and bloodstained Afro. They carried him away.

"He's one lucky nigger," Joey overheard the head maintenance man tell Drysdale. "He went between blades. Mostly, anyway. He's cut bad, and the leg's busted up, but there's nothing gone altogether." Within minutes, though the corrugator was silent, the grinding roar of machinery started again, and Drysdale told Joey to clear the mess of cardboard from the end of the corrugator. Joey heard him but said nothing; he just looked at the bloodstains on Drysdale's shirt and pants, and then walked away. He looked back to see Drysdale pull out his pocket watch. His hand shook as he opened the cover. Then he snapped it shut, cocked his arm ready to toss it at the corrugator, but stopped and stuck it back in his hip pocket.

Joey walked to the end of the corrugator, but he didn't stack any cardboard. He kicked the pile until he found the piece of William's bootlace. Then he walked off in the general direction of the men's room. He wanted to keep on walking all the way out the door, to the car, go home, wake Maggie, make love, and never come back. He passed Marty's workstation. The printer was idle without cardboard coming steadily from the corrugator. Marty was bent over sketching in his notepad and didn't notice Joey.

Rolling William's shoelace around his finger, as he opened the men's room door, Joey saw Scully hugging the toilet and retching. Joey stepped up to the urinal as Scully erupted again. Joey peed, then went to the sink and ran cold water over his hands. He was looking at the blood splotches on his own white tee shirt when Scully came to the other sink and ran water, too. Joey couldn't help staring through the mirror at the stub of Scully's right arm. For a while in first grade, they all believed that if you were touched by Celeste Ryan's stub, you'd lose your own arm and he remembered the glee in her eyes at the sudden power her deformity.

"What the fuck are you looking at?" growled Scully, splashing water on his face with his left hand.

"You've got puke on your shirt."

Joey shut the water off, flicked his two good hands dry and turned away. There was less than an hour to go. He pulled the piece of chartreuse shoelace from his pocket again and tied it in a loop. He slid the loop over his right hand onto his wrist, kicked the men's room door open and went back to work.

Newport News Shipbuilding and Drydock Strike 1999

Mary Franke

For Virgil Fairfield Large (1910-1977), who with a seventh grade education apprenticed at Newport News Shipyard and took me on Saturday mornings to see the ships he built.

Daddy I watched you
cough your life out
blood on your handkerchief

Daddy I watched you
work eighteen-hour days
seven day weeks during the war
Daddy I was with you when we went to the slums
head down times when they laid you off
Daddy I remember a million
little burn holes in your khaki work clothes
and in your skin
sometimes big ones oozing and scabbing.
Daddy you had to turn up the TV
because welding burnt out your ears
and your blue eyes brilliant as an acetylene flame
dulled into scarred earths
Daddy you drank like a man
and smoked Luckies because considering
your work that was not
the worst thing you could do . . .

Daddy when the union came
you were the first to join and I went too
it was too late for you
but not for my brothers and me
Daddy you fell three hundred feet
down a drydock on your back
and got up—

Daddy when I stand with these men
and women on this line
who may not live to retire to Florida
who need health insurance who are
belittled by their employers

with the big paychecks employers
who do not drive sixty miles from
a North Carolina farm in an old car
Daddy when I stand with your sisters
and brothers of the union
I am still a woman of peace
against making weapons but not ships
—When I stand with these workers
I see them and I see you coughing
your life out into that handkerchief I see
all their little curly and straight-haired
children   the cocoa and the pineapple
the lemon sherbet and the butter
pecan   the peach-cicle sweeties
going to school   wanting ice cream
wanting to be smart
not death or poverty
and I see you Daddy
and I stand Daddy
I stand

Dead-Loss   David Mason

Rough seas must have killed the entire catch. Two holds of king crab lay rotting on the *Norseman's* deck, falling apart like wet rag dolls. The smell of decay filled the hull, and people on the lines talked: "Dead-loss. The *Norseman* come in loaded with dead."

"They should've taken better care."

"Sometimes there's nothing you can do about it."

Missy took the ladder up. She wanted not so much to see the crab boat tied alongside the ship's hull as to breathe fresh air. In the ladder's housing the smell was trapped, suffocating, so it was a relief to emerge on the deck even in darkness, and stand among worklights shining on wet booms and pallets. Rain blew sideways in the wind, as it had come for days.

Looking down on the *Norseman*, she saw Wheeler holding a handkerchief over his nose. He and his unloaders stood there stunned. There was nothing alive to bring up on the winch, so they stood around holding their noses. Lot of good it would do.

Wheeler had noticed her. He uncovered his face, looking up and waving with the balled-up handkerchief, as if she couldn't recognize him by his yellow rain gear with Get Stoned felt penned on the back, the crumpled sou'wester too small for his head, his limp blond ponytail hanging out in back.

Missy moved away from the gunwale. She didn't know why. She could always say the smell of dead-loss drove her back.

Rain sprayed as if from some giant hose, a heavy cold rain with all of winter behind it. She wore only her jeans, boots and longjohns top, and as she stood on the deck she felt her skin go cold and firm in the rain. The ship swayed under her like a whale shying from the touch of land.

It was a converted World War II Liberty Ship, tethered to shore, gutted of engines, a gutless floating factory and bunkhouse. Missy worked the lines inside, and most days after work she took the ladder up on deck to see where she was. These days it was always dark after work, but she could feel the bare-backed islands like a crowd of slumbering giants. She could name hills in the dark without a moon.

At work all day she heard people bitch about the Aleutians, bitch about cannery work. They shook their heads over Missy. *Poor kid don't know what she's missing. Honey, I got a man with two houses and trees in both yards. Only reason I'm up here's to keep paying on my car. I got a new Chevy with a sun roof. You don't even know what a sun roof's for. Missy don't even hear us, don't know what she's missing.*

"All I know is it's better than Kodiak," Missy told them. In Kodiak her Mom had to dance in the bars. She died of a heart condition when

Missy was sixteen. "I wanted to come out here," she told them. "Beats hell out of stripping."

Wheeler was like them, saving for a house. What good was a house? You got to be its slave. Owning a house is like standing under a leaky roof in the rain and tearing up hundred dollar bills. I like it here. I'm a free spirit. You just have your work and your free time, no complications.

But a dead-loss got to her. All that waste.

She went down by the companionway over what used to be the engine room. It was a catwalk down through the heat and stink of oil from the boilers and auxiliaries. In the gallery she poured a cup of coffee. Coffee makes life simple; you get wet or cold and it's all you need. Wheeler complicated everything. He would look at her with those wet dog eyes, always wanting her.

He'll hate me soon enough, she thought.

Her old man, Hank, sat at the big table in the galley, shuffling cards. He was still decked out in his stained cook's apron, though it was past supper and the galleyslaves were scrubbing down. He kept his cigarettes rolled up Navy style in the sleeve of his t-shirt. The tattoo on his right arm, under the cigarettes, had blurred because the tattoo chick in Seattle stuck the needle in too shallow or something. Hank was getting grey, pot-bellied. His mustache and the three hairs of a mole on his cheek were black, but the rest of his hair was silver as a fur seal's. He winked at Missy, and she moved behind him as he dealt five-card stud to the Filipinos. Tonight the Filipinos were winning and Hank was down, squeezing his cigarette flat in his lips.

He wasn't really her old man. She called him that because he lived a long time with her Mom. He was with her when she died, and after that he said he'd watch over Missy like her God damned Guardian Angel. Truth was, Missy took care of Hank, reminded him to wash his apron every now and then or comb his hair. She got him up each morning in time to cook breakfast for the peons, watched his drinking, told him to quit acting like a Shriner clown.

"Shouldn't play poker drunk."

Hank flicked his cigarette like Bogart. "Gotta lose sometime, sweetheart."

"Tell me about it."

A fisherman off the *Norseman* sat at a corner table. He looked close to thirty, and she could smell his Right Guard from fifteen feet away. Least he didn't smell like a dead crab. His big hands clamped a coffee cup, red hands with nails like scallop shells. Missy went over to him, the way she often did with guys she hardly knew. Like a test.

"Bad storm, eh?"

The fisherman set his coffee aside. He was blond like Wheeler, but bearded, with shallow lines on his forehead. He had the steady, exhausted look fishermen get near the season's end, as if it took a lot of effort to sit with his back straight. Until he spoke she thought he must be Norwegian.

"You work here?" he asked. Then he nodded, answering his own question: "Seen you around."

She sat at his table and they talked. His name was Chuck. He had a wife in Seattle but no kids. His short hair looked oily, probably from the hot shower he took after they tied up.

"How long you been in Alaska?"

"Forever," Missy said.

"What kind of work they got you doing?"

"I'm a floater. I go job to job where they need me."

He shook his head. "Drive me crazy. Don't know how you stand it."

Fishermen always asked how cannery workers could stand it. Missy bummed a cigarette, and Chuck went on: "I like to be on a boat that moves. Goes somewhere. Anywhere. Not anchored like this one. What do you do, pack meat?"

"Mostly."

"Drive me God damn crazy."

He looked away. But soon enough his eyes came back, and she knew they were trained on her chest. There were not many women on the ship.

She had seen him before, whenever the Norseman came in, but never talked to him until now. Hank used to kid her: "Missy likes her men experienced." He stopped kidding when she met Wheeler. "Now there's a hard-working boy, lead-man on a crew, and your age, almost. You could do a lot worse."

Two peons came into the galley for coffee. Chuck watched them, tilting his head, then leaned across the table at her. "These people are a bunch of puppets." He sat back, taking the cup and turning it in his big hands. "Are you a puppet too?"

"I got my own way to handle it."

"How do you handle it?"

He looked at her as if he were swallowing laughter.

"Just empty your mind," she said, "float, don't think about it. I'm that way about everything. I don't read the papers or write letters, either. That way nothing bothers me. Guys come up here who went to Viet Nam or Desert Storm. I don't want to hear all that stuff."

She wasn't sure he listened. By the flat look in his eyes she judged he had been days without sleep, but she knew his eyes were on her. She felt heavy from Hank's food, but not fat yet like some women. Wheeler told her she should eat more vegetables. He was always after the company to fly in a crate of lettuce more than once a week. Wheeler.

"You cold?"

"A little," she said. "I got wet outside."

"Want to go somewhere?"

She glanced at Hank. He was lost in his poker game, lighting a fresh cigarette with the old one's stub. "I got my own room in the bunkhouse," she said.

                    *   *   *

They left the ship by the gangplank and crossed the gravel road to the old shore bunkhouse in the rain and the weird glow of worklights.

Her mattress lay on the floor of her room, which smelled like wood and burlap. She had Chuck lie down, and gave him a massage.

"Strong hands," he said.

"I know what to do."

Afterwards they lay apart from each other. Missy listening for any stray sound. Chuck wouldn't stay. She made him out in the dark as he fished for his pants. "How old are you, anyway?"

"Twenty," Missy said.

"Liar. You're fresh out of high school."

"Never went to high school."

"I could get you out of here," he said. "Ever ride on a crab boat? Maybe I'll take you out."

"Who wants to ride on a boat all covered with dead crab?"

"They'll clean her up soon."

Missy sat up. "When can we go?"

"I'll come by sometime."

"What about your wife?"

"What about her?"

"You said you were married."

"That didn't make any difference just now, did it?"

"Maybe it did and maybe it didn't."

"Up here a guy's not married."

He wore clogs on his feet like the Norwegians did when they weren't working, and he slipped them on now as he finished tucking in his shirt.

"Are you married when you go to Seattle?"

"Sure I am. But up here I'm not. I don't lie about it. I'm no liar."

"I don't care what you do," Missy said. "Like I told you, I'm a floater."

"I'll stop by," Chuck said.

When he was gone Missy couldn't keep his face in her mind. It was too early to sleep, so she followed the smell of marijuana to a party down the hall. The grass helped her relax and forget about Chuck. Still, she couldn't stop thinking about Wheeler, and when she got back to her room it took her a long time to fall asleep.

*   *   *

Late that night something knocked her awake. The door knocking.

"It's me," Wheeler said. "Let me in. There's someting I got to say to you."

Missy let him knock.

"I know you're in there," he said. "I heard you were with some guy tonight."

Quiet. But he was still there, behind the door. Missy tightened her eyes.

"Asshole's probably bragging about it. Hey! Do you hear me?"

She lay quietly until he was gone.

*   *   *

In the morning it was hard to get out of bed. The thought of another day on the extraction line and not at sea on a crab boat made her feel sluggish. She put on her jeans, sniffed the pits of her longjohns top and decided it would do for another day, yanked on her boots and went out.

It was raining again. A dull glaze on the road's gravel. Pockmarks on the bay.

The foreman put her on the greenbelt, packing crab legs into trays for the freezer. She had put in an hour at this work—it was about seven-thirty—when Wheeler and the whole unloading crew went by in the companionway. He didn't stop, and she knew she was being ignored.

At coffee break, hanging up her apron by the galley door, she saw him again. He came up to her, sweating from the work of unloading a new boat. "How come you didn't answer me last night?"

"What do you mean?"

"I about knocked your door down."

"Did you? I must've slept through it."

Wheeler grabbed her arm, and she saw that his mouth was pressed shut in anger. He had a thin face. His ponytail had loosened and there were strands of blond hair stuck to his sweaty brow. Then his grip loosened, as if he couldn't remember what he grabbed her for. He stepped back, looking at her down the thin hook of his nose. "Okay," he said. "Okay, the hell with it. You got time? You want to smoke?"

"If you got one, I'll smoke it with you."

They took the steel steps down into the hot darkness of the old engine room. Wheeler reached inside his raincoat. He didn't bother to look around to see if anyone watched. Wheeler's joints were always these little, tightly-rolled works of art. He lit up, but let her have the first toke.

"You think I don't know," he said. "I'm not pissed. I know you want me to be, but I'm not."

She handed him the joint, making a show of holding in the smoke so she couldn't say aything.

"I never know if you're listening to me," Wheeler said. "I mean, what do you want? I'm knocking on your door like an idiot while this guy's on the Norseman fucking bragging about it."

"You're crazy."

"Don't you know the guy's married?"

"Who?"

Wheeler turned away. He bent over so he could straighten when he toked and get a rush. He passed the joint back. The rush or the heat made his face look redder, all out of shape. He wiped his forehead with a thin hand, reached back and shook out his ragged ponytail.

Missy had a buzz. "I don't know why you're so pissed off. I mean, it's not like I want to buy a house or nothing."

"What?"

"You're always talking about a house. LIke you want to buy a house."

"What the hell does that have to do with it?"

"It's like all I ever hear from you. How you're saving your money up for this house."

"I can't talk to you," Wheeler said. "You don't even try to talk. You fucking don't know how."

"I can't handle all that house crap," Missy said. But the next toke confused her. She saw him fighting sweat and frustration, and a side of her wanted to hold him, a little boy, feeding him love. When they met he was working the brine tank, freezing crab claws in salt water, and the salt dried his hands so much that cracks opened in the skin. She used to rub cream in them. He had such small hands. They trembled when he touched her.

"Hey," she said. "Don't be mad." She kissed him.

"I still love you," Wheeler said.

She laughed. Her head felt like a balloon. "What do you want? You want anything?"

"Did you hear what I said?"

"Don't be so serious."

"Jesus," he said. "I give up." He left her with the roach in her hand and took the steel steps two at a time until he was out of sight.

"Well don't go away mad." She giggled, then sat down on the steps feeling heavy and half sick.

Break time was over, but she went into the galley for coffee anyway. As she stood at the urn she got a friendly goose from Hank, who asked her what she did to get Wheeler so mad. She smelled booze on Hank's breath. "Nothing. How much did you lose last night?"

"Too much."

"Me and Wheeler broke up," Missy said. She didn't know where they came from, but tears burned the rims of her eyes. "I don't know. I guess he don't like the way I am or something."

"Hey," Hank said. "Papa's here."

*   *   *

Chuck stopped by whenever the *Norseman* was in port. If Missy was still on the line, he would take the key to her room and fall asleep on the mattress. Her room was warm. One window faced the steaming ship anchored across the road. The ship was painted grey, as if to match the weather of these islands. God made Dutch Harbor when he ran out of colors. Grey for the rock and patches of snow, a few rust spots for the heather. No trees. Trees were for places with deep soil.

When she and Wheeler first met he stapled burlap to the sheetrock of her walls, and this made the room smell like a home or what she imagined a clean barn would smell like. If there wasn't work to do, Missy could spend forever in that room.

Though she saw Wheeler in the galley or when his crew marched past the lines, they never talked. She head a rumor that he wanted to make up, so she avoided him, stopped going to the little dope parties after work because he might be there. Then she heard his contract was almost up, he was ready to fly out to Seattle. She didn't look for him; She didn't go to the airstrip on the day, didn't listen for the plane. His six months were up and he was gone. No more Get Stoned rain slicker. No more ponytail. You could fly out too, people told her. You got more months in here than anybody. The company owes it to you. "Not me," she said. "You won't find me in no Seattle."

Chuck came by one night with a full bottle of whisky, and when they'd finished half of it she said to him, "What about that ride you promised me?"

"What about it?"

"You said you'd take me out on your boat."

"We're still fishing."

"Not tonight you're not."

"Soon," he said. "When the season's over."

She gave him a massage again, and let him do whatever he wanted with her, and when he said it was time to go she held tight to him. "Tonight you're staying here."

He laughed, a big hand like a hat on her hair. "Why the hell not?"

*   *   *

In December it snowed heavily. There was a week when Chuck never came, and word had it the fishermen stayed out longer for the final catch of the season. On the ship they worked non-stop. It was a life of work and noise and sleep. Missy rarely had time to see the deck, but one night she went up alone to see the wet slabs of snow on the hatches. She tilted back her head and let flakes fall on her face.

After twelve hours on the line, or fifteen, she came back to her room, drank, fell asleep with the smell of warm burlap and whisky. She could never want anything more. Maybe she didn't even want Chuck to come back. It would only complicate her life. She felt like one of those Japanese soldiers she'd heard about who never knew the war was over; they burrowed deeper and deeper into their islands out in the Pacific, and finally someone came along with a camera and took their picture and told them they didn't have to eat rat meat any more.

Hell, you don't have to know who's president to be happy. Does it matter if it's Clinton or somebody else? Does it matter if they're fighting a war somewhere? Nobody's fighting nothing up here. There's nothing to fight but the weather and your own ghost.

Some nights she got drunk with Hank. He borrowed from her pay- checks to stay in the poker games, and bought her drinks to say thanks. But those Filipinos had a way of winning. They had a language of their own, and a way of squinting over their cards. You couldn't beat them.

"What do I need money for?" Missy said to Hank. "What am I gonna do, buy a house?"

When he got real drunk Hank wanted to talk about her Mom, and Missy didn't want to hear about all that. She didn't want to hear about the night it happened or what a good person her mom was in spite of what people said.

Sometimes she heard rumors about Wheeler. There was talk he'd found a fishing job for next season with a full crew share. He was going to Kodiak. Rumor had it he was fed up with Dutch Harbor.

The night Chuck came back Missy was drinking alone in her room. He opened the door without knocking, leaned in and looked around until he found her there in the shadows. She stood up. They met for a hug on the mattress. He felt as stiff as a piece of driftwood and said yes, she could rub his back for a while. "Can't stay long, though. We got some work to do on the boat."

"Can't work while they're unloading."

"We're third in line. It'll be tomorrow night before they unload."

"Then do I get my ride?"

"Sure thing, Missy. I told you I'd take you out. Maybe some of the guys'll come along."

"No, just you and me."

"If you say so."

"And no talk about your wife?"

"Do I ever talk about my wife?"

"No, but I want to make sure."

When he had left, Missy lay alone on her mattress. She heard the hard snow chattering to the roof, dreamed snow was human, a man coming down the bunkhouse hallway, just outside, just a few feet away....

*   *   *

The next night Chuck came in roaring drunk. He kicked open her door and came in holding a bottle of tequila like a baseball bat, swung it lightly to touch her stomach as she stood barefoot on the mattress. "Home run. Hey, little girl, give me a kiss."

Missy wrapped her arms around his neck. He was so tall she had to stand on her toes, and she rubbed her forehead in his beard.

"Brung a buddy of mine along, okay?" He unhooked her arms and turned to the door. "Missy, meet Babe. I told him about you."

Babe stepped in. He was short, dark-bearded and shy.

"He won't hurt you," Chuck said. "He's my best buddy."

She had never seen Chuck this drunk; he could hardly stand up. And already this Babe guy had crouched on her mattress, looking up at Chuck like catcher to pitcher, like *What's the signal here?* Missy glanced at the door, but Chuck stepped over and closed it. He unscrewed the cap of his tequila bottle, titled back his head and filled his mouth.

Babe untied the laces of his boots.

"I thought we could relax together," Chuck said.

"Not tonight."

"Why not?" He took her hand, led her away from the door. "Hey, don't be scared. We're friends. Babe's a good head." He set the bottle on the floor, waved his hand over it like a magic wand to make sure it stood by itself. "It's like I'm worried about you. Didn't I say I always tell the truth? Nobody's fooling anybody here. Season's over, so I got to go for a while. Nothing I can do about it. Can't change the ticket. But I started thinking who's going to take care of you."

His voice sounded hollow, as if it came from far away.

Missy didn't know how she made her next move, or the one after it. Only that Chuck sat against the door, drinking. He watched or dozed. She could feel him at her back while Babe undid her buttons, then she felt Babe's mouth at her breasts. The way Babe whispered, "I'm sorry," over and over.

When the two men were asleep she heard the snow coming back, chattering over the bunkhouse roof. Babe's breath was sour on her skin. She waited for the time when they would be gone. Both of them. More than anything she wanted them to go away. Just leave her alone. It would be like floating.

She lay there quietly. Sound of snow coming down the hall.

Poem for a Friend in Prison   A.D. Winans

hello, Joe
I could handle the name change
but they keep transferring you
to so many different units
that I'm running out of space
in my address book
and now they're shuttling you
from prison to prison
I know this is america
but this is a bit too much
even for a pro like me
all these prisons being built
like factory assembly lines
I mean there's only so many
license plates one can make
makes no sense to me

you ask how I'm doing
which is kind of you
given your circumstances
I'm confined to my own prison
even if there are no keepers
where life has become a surreal movie
with nothing but bit actors
like those old time sing-a-longs
they flashed on the movie screen
when I was a kid
follow the bouncing ball
but I can't and couldn't then
carry a note

It's a hard life brother
on the inside on the outside
today it's Kosovo
tomorrow New York City

part of the trouble lies with the judges
who must be poor mathematicians
when it comes to handing out time

and what the fuck is the world coming to
when poets shun writing for e-mail?

the old man down on market street
the one with no legs and a skate board
has more moxy than the president
and the sob sister media crying
about the likes of Monica Lewinsky

this is a bitch of a poem
not a bitching one
I know you know the difference
even if the jailers don't
those count dracula look-alikes
thirsting after your blood
stepping on over and around
dead bodies
looking for live spirits to bury

I wish I could tell you there's
light at the end of the tunnel
but there isn't
the new Governor believes
in capital punishment
as if death were a spanking
or being sent to bed without supper
got to get me a new dictionary
the one I have must have belonged
to Bill Clinton with all
its tortured definitions

The message of America can't be found
on Mount Rushmore
it's written in blood at the Texas
Book Depository

I know a guy who believes
if we reduce the world population
by a third and close our borders
there would be enough food for everyone
in the world
too much breeding he said

but this same man breeds killer dogs
and has six kids and another on the way
it's the kind of shit that's driving me sane
just when I was getting the insane part
down to perfection

I feel like I'm the lone survivor
standing on the deck of the Titanic
destined to walk the ocean floor
with a fish womb view of reality
better watch it brother
you might get what you wish for
a new trial a new judge a new jury
but would the outcome be any different?

the D.A. should wear a black robe
a wig and powder his cheeks
bend over and beg forgiveness
what's left of Eliot Ness' gang busters
could take on the wise guys
outside the court house
hell, I might even buy a ticket
mouth a few obscenities
to take the edge off the hype

we are born we die
we spend time in between
be it behind or outside the walls
and the stock market keeps going up
and the prisons keep getting built
and all I can do about it is write
these "bitching" poems to an audience
who does nothing but bitch

sometimes I think I'm a retarded
space alien put here by a superior race
you on the inside me on the outside
inner parts of a human computer waiting
to be blanked from the screen

ORIZABA! Dave Roskos

I

The sea which
fed him his
livelihood
swallowed
him whole

foot caught
in the rigging
of the lobster
nets

overboard
like Hart Crane

ORIZABA!

II

Hart Crane
eaten by
sharks;

poem-circled.

scent of blood
& bone—

not very lyrical,
not much music
in it.

The Miracle of the Northern Lights   **Maj Ragain**

Five years ago, kudzu cancer had climbed
Billy's backbone, tumors threading his ribcage
as if he were a trellis to be overrun.
When he could no longer walk, Billy rolled around Kent
in his wheelchair, one end of town to the other,
sometimes all night, singing and weeping,
as if to cast out the demons
who were eating his heart.
He renounced the chemo, its slow burn,
pulled the plug and holed up in his trailer.

A couple of years later, he walked up to me
in the Brady cafe, hugged me hard and said
'God bless you, brother.' He meant it,
calling down God's blessing on me where I stood.
'I'm alive because I gave it all to Jesus.'
No doubt what it was. In that moment
I believed in him, in Jesus, in the blood that redeems,
the cavalcade of miracles, the stigmata,
the dancing bones of the saints,
the lady of Guadalupe hovering in the air above us.
Billy's eyes crackled with sweet love from nowhere.

Today, I found Billy in the Hills department store
parking lot, pushing a flotilla of twenty or so
carts to the front door, all wedged inside one another,
his knees bent for leverage.
His orange vest marked him as an employee,
not a homeless shopping cart pilgrim.
After he had wrangled the herd of carts
through the sliding doors, he came back
for a maverick at the lot's far corner.
I drove up to him and offered my hand.
Billy was still happy, that borealis light in his eyes,
still sunkissed by his blessing,
smiling like Lazarus on a spring morning.
When I told him I was driving to Oregon
to visit my son, Billy's eyes filled with rivers,
the Rouge, the Willamette, the Columbia,
with mountains, the Cascades.

Billy had lived there for a year,
in a national forest consorting with bears,
eating peeled bark, boiling snow.
Would I say hello to the rivers,
to the mountains for him.
You bet I will.
We shook hands. He blessed me again.
You must have it to give it.
It is the brush of unseen lips.
It is a pillar of fire.

Billy is here to teach me how to live,
as bends to his work, this shepherd of the carts.
Hopeful beanstalk to heaven carts.
Silver fill this bucket with faith carts.
Beaded rosary, hail mary mother of grace carts.
Devil go back to hell carts, satan you can't catch me carts.
Everything is holy carts, bind the wounds of the children carts.
Cross the river styx carts, final clearance red tag carts.
Fly with me to heaven carts, storewide savings moonlight madness carts.
Brother take a load off and put it right on me carts.
The body is more than discounted raiment carts.
The life is more than meat on sale carts.
Don't leave your soul unattended carts.
Love outlives death carts, take me into your chest
like burning coals carts, whirling dervish be still carts.
You don't need a machine to breathe carts.
Four wheeled follow the star to baby Jesus carts.

Death cannot find a seat on Billy's silver train
across this desert of asphalt.
Sweet Billy, blessed by his blessing.
Billy, let me ride.

Grist for the Mill   Mary E. Weems

Inside the mill steel, walk, and talk
are one motion. Like conversations curl
from lines and machines like steam
and temperature is always summer. Men
hum the background music from the *Wizard of Oz*
"Ho ee oh hoo o, ho ee oh hoo o," identical
movements pile up like nobodies, nameless days
assemble in a world where gray is the favorite color.
One man reads Baraka between beats, moves
the wrong way, talks too fast, laughs on the way
home, but the heart of the mill stands like a
lighthouse on fire.

Their spirits are grist, the pretty-flame outsiders see,
the burn-off for steel   mill   owners
and their wives.

CREDITS—BIOGRAPHICAL SKETCHES

Paul Allen (Charleston, SC) teaches poetry writing, writing song lyrics, and freshman composition at the College of Charleston. He also co-edits Crazyhorse. His first collection, American Crawl, received the Vassar Miller Poetry Prize (UNT Press) and his second is forthcoming from Salmon Publishing Ltd. in Ireland. Allen also has a CD entitled The Man with the Hardest Belly: Poems & Songs. Both book and CD are available at amazon.com. Allen's idea of heaven is St. Peter's allowing him to watch as certain souls, in their bid to get in, try to explain the logic and humanitarianism of the trickle down theory of economics.

Maggie Anderson (Kent, OH) was born in New York City and moved to West Virginia when she was thirteen years old. She has taught in creative writing programs at the University of Pittsburgh, the Pennsylvania State University, the University of Oregon, Hamilton College, and now teaches at Kent State University where she directs the Wick Poetry Program. She spent many years teaching in the writer-in-the-schools programs in Ohio and West Virginia. She has received a fellowship from the National Endowment for the Arts, the Ohio Arts Council, and the Pennsylvania Council on the Arts. Her most recent book is *Windfall: New and Selected Poems* (University of Pittsburgh 2000).

David Budbill (Wolcott, VT) was born in Cleveland, Ohio in 1940. He is the author of six books of poems, eight plays, a children's book, and two works of fiction for young adults, and a libretto for opera. He has received a Guggenheim Fellowship in poetry and a National Endowment for the Arts Fellowship in play writing. He also performs his writing accompanied with jazz. Recent books include *Moment to Moment: Poems of a Mountain Recluse* (Copper Canyon Press) and *Judevine* (Chelsea Green Publishing, writing about an impoverished Vermont town.

Nan Byrne (Virginia Beach, VA) has worked hard for the money since the age of fifteen. The child of Irish-American parents she was raised in a working class neighborhood in New York where her jobs included house cleaner, industrial worker and supermarket checker. In recent years she has been laboring in the knowledge factory. An MFA graduate of Virginia Commonwealth University and the author of *Uncertain Territory* she is currently at work on a screenplay. New poems can be found in the *Seattle Review, Sulphur River Literary Review*, and *So to Speak: A Feminist Journal of Language and Art.*

Dane Cervine (Santa Cruz, CA) serves as Chief of Children's Mental Health in Santa Cruz, California, where he works with families in need. He firmly believes poetry must better address the struggles and joys of society if it is to have meaning beyond the personal—be rooted in the ground of public life. Dane's poems in this theme are forthcoming in *Raven Chronicles, & Out Of Line,* as well as work recently appearing in *POEM, Lucid Stone, Urban Spaghetti, Rockhurst Review, Studio One,* among others. The new anthology *To Love One Another: Poems Celebrating Marriage*, from Grayson Books, includes one of his latest.

Wanda Coleman (Marina del Rey, CA) "Recipe for WANDA COLEMAN: Take 18 years in the racist Los Angeles School System during the 50s-60s, add a thatch of hair that always goes back to Africa and a body that bursts all seams, stir in a tablespoon of allergic dermatitis, a pinch of honesty, a cup of chopped integrity and a half pint of Edgar Allen Poe. Refrigerate in the Mojave overnight. Roll out on asphalt. Spread thick with a paste of disappointment, sensitivity and misguided loyalty. Roll up carefully, slice, and place gently on stainless still pan. Roast for 30-odd years. Enjoy while appreciating fine art and wine." She has poems in *Antioch Review, New Bones: Contemporary Black Writers in America,* and *The Outlaw Bible of American Poetry.* Recent books include *Bathwater Wine,* winner of the 1999 Lenore Marshall Poetry Prize, *Mambo Hips & Make Believe* (a novel), and *Mercurochrome: New Poems* (Black Sparrow Press). She is featured in *African American Writers: Portraits and Visions* by Lynda Koolish (University Press of Mississippi) © 2001.

John Cottle (Electic, AL) lives on Lake Martin in Central Alabama with his wife Nancy, and practices law in a small town nearby where he represents the working people who inspire his stories. He writes in his spare time and is currently working on a novel. He has previously been published in *Amaryllis*, won a Hackney Literary Award for 2001 and was a finalist in the short story category of the William Faulkner Creative Writing Competition 2001.

Christopher Cunningham (College Park, GA) says, "I write on a typewriter in a crumbling old house by a window facing the humid southern night. I believe that poetry is a line cook during a busy rush, a grin from beneath the beard of a homeless guy, and three days off in a row." His two chapbooks of poetry are: *Screaming in Some Beauty* (Four-Sep Publications, 2001) and *18 Blue Collar Abstractions* (Cannedphlegm Press 2002). He is thirty-two.

Nelson Demery, III (New Orleans, LA) received his M.F.A. from the University of New Orleans, and he is currently enrolled in the Ph.D. program in creative writing at the University of Houston. Mr. Demery is also a Cave Canem Fellow and a member of the NOMMO Literary Society. His poems have been featured on "All Things Considered," a program broadcast by National Public Radio.

Becky Dickerson (Huron, OH) is a graduate of the School of Art at Bowling Green State University. She works in the photo studio and teaches photography. Her work with migrant and farm labor was featured in *Getting By: Stories of Working Lives* (Bottom Dog Press).

John Olivares Espinoza (Indio, CA) son to former Mexican migrant workers, he spent his youth landscaping with his father and brothers for the upper-middle class affluent. John received his BA in Creative Writing and Sociology from the University of California, Riverside. He is the author of two chapbooks: *Gardeners of Eden* (Chicano Chapbook Series, 2000) and *Aluminum Times* (Swan Scythe Press, 2002). Twice nominated for a Pushcart Prize, his awards include a Paul and Daisy Soros Fellowship for New Americans. He currently teaches poetry to underprivileged children around rural areas in Arizona.

Allen Frost (Bellingham, WA) was born in La Jolla, Ca., and grew up in Seattle. He has worked at a variety of jobs and is now a library clerk at Western University of Washington in Bellingham where he lives with his wife and daughter. His book of fiction *Ohio Trio* appeared from Bottom Dog Press.

Mary Franke (Norfolk, VA) was born in the shipyard town of Portsmouth, Virginia, married in her mid-teens and earned her high school equivalency diploma. Admitted to college during open admissions in the 1960s, she is an activist for feminism, peace, race, and housing. She is retired. She has three children and a granddaughter. Her work has appeared in *Calyx, Hecate, Off Our B*acks, and two anthologies. She has performed on radio television, coffeehouses, conferences, homeless shelters, and at activist rallies over the last twenty years. She is vice president of Partisan Press and co-editor of the *Blue Collar Review*.

Jonathan Hayes (San Francisco,CA) has worked hard for the money at various jobs — from cannery worker to apple picker — in order to survive as a wandering American poet. He is a student in the creative writing department at San Francisco State University. He is the author of *Echoes from the Sarcophagus* (3300 Press, 1997) and *St. Paul Hotel* (Ex Nihilo Press, 2000). He edits the literary/art *magazine Over the Transom.*

Diana Joseph (Grand Junction, CO) was born and raised in western Pennsylvania. She's bussed tables in a smorgasbord, worked at a pizza parlor, in a strawberry field, a pallet shop, a public library, and as a waitress and short order cook. She currently lives in Grand Junction, Colorado, where she edits Pinyon Press and teaches creative writing at Mesa State College. Her short story collection, *Happy or Otherwise*, is forthcoming from Carnegie Mellon University Press.

Thea S. Kuticka (Tempe, AZ) has worked as a landscaper, barista, and waitress. She dropped out of her stenography classes when she was twenty and went on to receive an MFA degree from the University of Virginia, despite her mother's urgings to "Just join the goddamn army." She received the Arizona Commission on the Arts fellowship and works as an editor at the Bilingual Press in Arizona. Recent works have appeared in *ACM, Alaska Quarterly Review,* and *Pacific Review*.

Jim Lang (Cleveland, OH) is a photographer/poet who has worked in newspaper, magazine, and small press publishing for 40 years. "I was born in the 40's, died in the 50's, thrived in the 60's, loved in the 70's, coasted in the 80's, predicted the 90's, reprises in the 2-K's." He has taught at universities, high and grade schools, and hung his work at galleries from Columbus to Toronto. "Read, showed off, & slept on walls & floors & lawns from sea to shining sea."

Mac Lojowsky (Cleveland, OH) has worked as a dishwasher, a gas station attendant, a painter, a journalist, a shit-shoveler, a city maintenance worker, a fruit picker, a state park ranger and a demolition man. He currently resides in California's Sespe Mountains and works as a house carpenter. As a rule, he doesn't trust folks with soft hands.

Fred Lonidier (La Jolla, CA) Associate Professor of Visual Arts at University of California at San Diego, member of University Council-FT Local 2034. He was born in La Jolla, California, and graduated from Yuba College, San Francisco State College, and University of California at San Diego. His work focusing on America's working poor has been exhibited widely.

Lenard D. Moore (Raleigh NC) the oldest of seven siblings, was born in Jacksonville, North Carolina. Growing up in rural Onslow County, he chopped weeds in his great-grandmother Fannie Simmons' peanut and cornfields. He spent most of his boyhood summers priming and hanging tobacco, picking blueberries and gardening. He has taught his daughter the art of gardening. He has served three years (1978-1981) as an Administrative Specialist/Postal Clerk in the United States Army. He has earned a B.A. (Magna Cum Laude) from Shaw University. He has also earned an M.A. in English and African American Literature from NC A&T State University. His poetry, essays and reviews have appeared in more than 350 publications. He is the author of *FOREVER HOME* (St. Andrews College Press, 1992). His chapbook, *GATHERING AT THE CROSSROADS*, is forthcoming from Red Moon Press, in 2002. He teaches English and world literature at Shaw University.

David Mason (Woodland Park, CO) grew up in Bellingham, Washington, and worked in Dutch Harbor, Alaska, as a young man. He has also lived in Greece and many parts of the United States, and for a time made his living as a gardener, house painter and odd-job man. He now teaches at the Colorado College and lives in the mountains outside Colorado Springs with his wife, Anne Lennox, a photographer. His work has appeared in such periodicals as *The Hudson Review, The Irish Times, The Sewanee Review, POETRY*, and *Shenandoah*. Books of poems include *The Buried Houses* and *The Country I Remember*, from Story Line Press. With the late John Frederick Nims he edited *Western Winds: An Introduction to Poetry*. His book of essays, *The Poetry of Life and The Life of Poetry*, appeared in 2000.

Suzanne Nielsen (Minneapolis, MN) grew up in St. Paul's East Side, a working class community, the setting for most of her short stories. She is known to be compulsive in many areas of her life, including writing genres. She writes poetry, fiction, essays, screenplays and memoir. She teaches writing at Metropolitan State University and her work has appeared in various literary magazines in all-of-the-above genres. In addition to teaching, Suzanne is a wife and mother, as well as the owner of two dogs. She grabs time whenever she can to create because if she isn't creating, she isn't happy. Suzanne firmly believes nothing is more truthful than the writing of fiction.

Maj Ragain (Kent, OH) lives along the Cuyahoga River where he teaches crative writing at Kent State University. A poet and prose writer, he frequently appears at coffeehouses, bookstores, and campuses. In the summer of 2001 he held a fellowship at the Fine Arts Work Center in Provincetown, MA. His most recent collection is *Twist the Axe: A Horseplayer's Story, Poems and Journal* (Bottom Dog Press 2001).

Wayne Rapp (Columbus, OH) was born on the Mexican border in the small mining town of Bisbee, Arizona. The location is not unlike San Pedro, where the dry snow would find its way into the cracks of the old wooden houses. His ancestry is mixed as is fairly common on the border. He traces his Mexican roots to the state of Sonora and his anglo background to Germany and Kentucky. Wayne's fiction has appeared in various publications including *High Plains Literary Review, Grit, Thema, Chiricú, The Americas Review,* and *VeriTales.* His fiction has twice been honored with Individual Artist Fellowships from the Ohio Arts Council and has been nominated for the Pushcart Prize. He is currently working on a collection of border stories.

Victoria Rivas (Waterbury, CT) is a poetry addict who supports her habit by programming computers. She has featured around Connecticut and New York, including the Knitting Factory in New York City. Her poems have been published in many journals and she has published one chapbook of her poetry, *Small Victories.* Victoria was on the organizing committees for the 1997 and the 2001 Connecticut Poetry Festivals and hosts a monthly reading at Barnes & Noble. She fills the rest of her time practicing and teaching Tang Soo Do, adjusting to married life for the third time, and raising her two stepchildren.

David Roskos (Manasquan, NJ) "Born: 10/24/64; New Jersey. Wrote to Allen Ginsberg in early 1980's (late teens); A.G. wrote back: 'Stay off Dope! Read William Carlos Williams complete works for grounding.' Some College. Dropped out. Started The Proletkult Poetry Circus (or Series) at The Court Tavern, in New Brunswick (NJ) in March 1986. Drugs. Worked mostly as a furniture mover; also as a "light industrial temp," plumber's helper, electrician's helper, hod-carrier, resident assistant in a Catholic Charities Men's homeless Shelter, janitor, etc. Edited & published first issue of *Big Hammer Magazine* in 1988, put Iniquity Press/Vendetta Books into motion. First chapbook, *The Energy of the Flesh* 1989. More drugs. Stints of abstinence. Pregnancy. Married in Vegas (divorced in Freehold). Ayler Windell Roskos born on Wm Blake's birthday, in 1996. Fatherhood. No more drugs. Work. Renewed focus into Press, publish *Big Hammers*; edited 5 issues of *Big Hammer Mag*, 1 issue of *Ball Peen Mag*, 2 issues of *N.J. Bowel & Bladder Control* (Mag), & around 25 other chapbooks, by various writers, on Iniquity Press/Vendetta Books. Was a regular contributor to *Dionysos, the Journal of Literature & Addiction*, in its most recent incarnation, under editorship of Jim Harbaugh, at University of Seattle's now defunct Addictions Studies Program.

Ben Satterfield (Hville, GA) is a former probation officer whose fiction, poetry, drama, reviews, and commentary have appeared in scores of periodicals from the literary Oxford Magazine and HIgh Plains Literary Review to mystery and men's magazines, and more critical articles have appeared in national journals: Poets & Writers and Studies in American Fiction. A disaffected university professor, he has also written on the abasement of education in this country, deploring what he calls the "edutainment" of today's teeming students. Born in North Carolina, an adopted Texan, he currently lives in central Georgia.

Trina Scordo (Ashbury Park, NJ)Trina Scordo grew up in northern New Jersey in a working class Italian family. She resides in the seaside town of Asbury Park, NJ where she runs the Shore Poets reading series and manages the New Jersey online poetry calendar. New Jersey's industrial landscape and Asbury's abandoned amusement buildings serve as her inspiration. She has been published in several anthologies including Beginnings Literary Magazine, Long Shot and Big Hammer. She is forthcoming in the Edison Literary Review and Echo in the Throat.

Irene Sedeora, (Morton, IL) After becoming a widow in her late twenties with a baby and a toddler, Irene Sedeora completed her college education. She later remarried and taught school briefly before having another child and becoming a full time homemaker. During a one-year stay in Singapore with her engineer husband and family, Sedora wrote a novel (which remains unpublished). Taking a creative writing course at a community college led to her first poem being published in *Skylark* (Purdue University Calumet). With the children now grown she fully devotes time to writing. Her publishing credits include *Dust & Fire* 2002, *The Good Foot Magazine, The Writer, Blue Collar Review, DownState Story, Mid-America Poetry Review, Our Bundle of Joy* (Meadowbrook Press 2001), and *Love Poems for the Media Age* (Ripple Effect Press, 2001).

Amber Shields, (Minneapolis, MN) is a senior at the University of Minnesota. She is majoring in French Studies and English and hopes to follow a career in translation after graduation. Amber's interest in writing poetry began several years ago when she read Anne Sexton's poem "I Remember."

Steven Skovensky (Chicago, Illinois) is a case manager with Lakefront SRO, a supportive housing agency. He graduated from Kent State University in Ohio and has been a frequent reader at poetry readings in the Kent, Cleveland, and Akron areas. Since moving to Chicago in 1999, he has been a featured reader at the Hungry Brain, Myopic Books and the Bucktown Arts Festival. He loves the Chicago River but often dreams of the Cuyahoga. In his current job, he leads a creative writing group for formerly homeless and low-income tenants. Delmar Press published their first book, *Whispers in the Dark, Voices in the Light,* in December, 2001

Minton Sparks (Nashville, TN) is a poet, teacher, and mother. Her poems call across the back fences of time. Sparks travels extensively, performing at various women's colleges sharing her unique brand of poetry. She graduated from Vanderbilt University in 1991 with a M.Ed. in Human Development Counseling. Her poems appear in literary journals like *the Clackamas Literary Review*, and *Lonzie's Fried Chicken.* Awarded the "Leonard Bernstein Fellowship" in 1998, Sparks soon began to teach poetry within the Tennessee high school system, offering classes funded by the fellowship. From 1990 to 2002, she has worked as adjunct professor of Psychology at Tennessee State University. Minton appeared on National Public Radio's *Weekend All Things Considered,* the internationally syndicated *WoodSongs Old-Time Radio Hour,* and *Exoterica, the Music and Poetry Festival* in the Bronx.

Sandra Lee Stillwell (Benicia, CA) is a native Californian, a descendant of the Karuk Tribe. Working for California State Parks allows her to view nature as it happens. She has written poetry for over 25 years. Her work has appeared in many small publications, as well as six anthologies and has won several awards.

Melvin Sterne (Davis, CA) worked union construction with the Boilermakers and the Ironworkers for 25 years. He earned his BA in English at the University of Washington, and is currently working on his MA in Creative Writing at the University of California at Davis. His stories and poems have appeared in *interSECTIONS*, *the Licton Springs Review*, *Furrow*, *Amarillo-Bay Magazine*, and *In Posse Review*. He was the winner of the 2001 Frank O'Connor Short Story Award (Auburn University), placed second in the 2001 William Faulkner Short Story Award (Tallahatchie RiverFest), and placed second in the HWYL/Diversity Incorporated Undergraduate Fiction Award (University of Wisconsin, Madison). He has work forthcoming in *Concrete Wolf*, and an essay about writing forthcoming in a textbook entitled *A Closer Look* (Sid Dobrin and Anis Bawarshi, eds; McGraw Hill, publisher).

Buddy Struble (Denton, TX) works for the *North Texas Review* and *American Literary Review*. His poems have most recently appeared in *Diner, NTR,* and the *Red Door Review*.

Thom Tammaro (Moorhead, MN) grandson of Italian immigrants, was born and raised in the heart of the steel valley of western Pennsylvania. He is the author of When the Italians Came to My Home Town and Minnesota Suite, collections of poems. He has co-edited three award-winning anthologies: *Visiting Emily: Poems Inspired by the Life and Work of Emily Dickinson* (2000, University of Iowa Press), *Imagining Home: Writing from the Midwest* (1995), and *Inheriting the Land: Contemporary Voices from the Midwest* (1993) both published by the University of Minnesota Press.

John Thompson (Media, PA) lives with his wife, Jayne, a writer, and two, sometimes three, cats. His work has appeared in Northeast Corridor, Piedmont Literary Review, Daedalus and Widener Review. He did, in fact, work a box factory's corrugator, one of too many jobs that were at times brutal, tedious or both, though as anyone who as ever worked at the wrong end of corrugator would attest, the corrugator is its own special kind of hell. He now tutors writing and rehabs houses, but still occasionally takes on almost any kind of work for a buck when necessary.

Will Watson (Long Beach, MS) born into the third generation of a family of steelworkers, worked in Northern Indiana plants for eight years before starting college on a bet in 1980, just before Dutch Reagan fired every single highly paid union air traffic controller in America. Sensing that highly paid union steelworkers might be next, Watson unexpectedly stayed in college long enough to emerge, somewhat shaken, with three degrees, the last a Ph.D in English from LSU. He is currently Associate Professor of English at the University of Southern Mississippi-Gulf Coast.

In his spare time he organizes for the Green Party and researches how people live without pirogies in Mississippi.

Cherelyn M. Willet (Fresno, CA) is a mom and wife who works part-time as an English instructor at Madera Community College and full-time cleaning house and trying to make ends meet. Her work was recently selected for honorable mention in *Anthology* magazine's 2001 poetry contest and she is putting together her first book of poems, which has yet to find a publisher. In June 2003 she will receive her MFA in Creative Writing, poetry emphasis, from Antioch University LA, and begin evading student loan repayment.

A. D. Winans (San Francisco, CA) is a graduate of San Francisco University and the former editor/publisher of Second Coming Magazine and Press. He is the author of numerous poetry books. His book *Holy Grail: Charles Bukowski and the Second Coming Revolution* detailing his friendship with the late Charles Bukowski has been published by Dust Books. A book of his *Selected Poems* has been translated into Serbian/Croation and will be published in Belgrade. Forthcoming: *A Bastard Child With No Place to Go* (12 Gauge Press).

(photo by Kat Nyberg)   (photo by Jim Lang)

The Editors

Larry Smith (Huron, OH) is a native of the industrial Ohio Valley at Mingo Junction, Ohio. He comes from a family of railroaders, farmers, and educators. He has taught at Firelands College of Bowling Green State University for 30 years and is the founder and director of Bottom Dog Press and the Firelands Writing Center. He has received a Fulbright lectureship to Italy and a Individual Artist Fellowship from the Ohio Arts Council as a critic. Smith is a biographer of Kenneth Patchen and Lawrence Ferlinghetti, and the author of *Milldust and Roses: Memoirs* (Ridgeway Press, 2002). He has co-edited the following anthologies for Bottom Dog Press in the Our Working Lives Series: *A Red Shadow of Steel Mills: Labor Poems and Photos,Getting By: Stories of Working Lives, Writing Work: Writers on Working-Class Writing*. He and his wife, Ann, live along Lake Erie.

Mary E. Weems (Cleveland, OH) is a native Clevelander, a performance poet, playwright, activist artist educator, and an adjunct English faculty in the English department, and at First College, both at Cleveland State University. Ms. Weems earned a Ph.D. in Education with a concentration in the integration of the arts and the urban public school curriculum, at the University of Illinois, Urbana-Champaign. She has published three short collections of poetry: *white* (Kent State University Press, 1996), *Fembles* (*The Heartlands Today*, 1996), and *Blackeyed*, (Burning Press, 1994). Her children's play (grades 4 – 8) *Move to the Back of the Bus,* has been produced by Young Audiences of Greater Cleveland for the last four years (1999 – 2002). In 1998, her play *Another Way to Dance*, won the Cleveland Public Theater's Chilcote Award for the Most Innovative Play by an Ohio Playwright. In 1998, her one-woman show *To Be or Not to Be in the 90s* was produced by the Cleveland Public Theater. In 1995, a book and video project titled *Off the Page*, in which she was the Artistic Director, co-editor, and one of the performers, won the Ohio Board of Regents' W.E.B. DuBois Award for community service. She has performed and/or conducted creative writing/performance based workshops in venues all over the country. Her work has appeared in several anthologies including: *Spirit & Flame: An Anthology of Contemporary African American Poets* (Syracuse University Press) and *Boomer Girls* (Iowa University Press). Weems' educational text comprised of scholarship, poetry, and two plays, developed from her dissertation *Publication and the Imagination-Intellect: I Speak from the Wound in my Mouth* is forthcoming from Peter Lang in 2003.

Acknowledgements & Permissions

"Felon," "Tis Morining Makes Mother a Killer,""Bad,"by Wanda Coleman from IMAGOES, Black Sparrow Press, Santa Rosa, California; copyright © 1983 by Wanda Coleman; reprinted with permission of the author.

"Long Story" is from Windfall, by Maggie Anderson , © 2000. Reprinted by permission of the University of Pittsburgh.

"Sorrow Knows this Dress" by Minton Sparks was first published in the *Clackamas Literary Review*/Fall/Winter 2001)

"Anson" by David Budbill, reprinted from *Judevine*, White River Junction, VT: Chelsea Green Publising.

"Farm Work" and "From the Field" by Leonard D. Moore were previously published in the author's book, *FOREVER HOME* (St. Andrews College Press, 1992). Originally appeared in *International Poetry Review*. "Working Class" by Leonard D. Moore was previously published on page 43 of the anthology, *IDENTITY LESSONS: Contemporary Writing About Learning to Be American* (Penguin Books, 1999).

"Sick Child" by Diana Joseph from a book of stories, *Happy or Otherwise*, to be published by Carnegie-Mellon Press 2003.

We are indebted to the photography of Fred Lonidier, Becky Dickerson, and Jim Lang, who also designed the book's cover.

Bottom Dog Press
P.O. Box 425
Huron, Ohio 44839
lsmithdog@aol.com
http://members.aol.com/lsmithdog/bottomdog
Fax: 419-433-9696

Working Lives Series

Robert Flanagan. *Loving Power: Stories.* 1990
0-933087-17-9 $8.95
A Red Shadow of Steel MIlls: Photos and Poems. 1991
(Includes Timothy Russell, David Adams, Kip Knott, Richard Hague)
0-933087-18-7 $8.95
Chris Llewellyn. *Steam Dummy & Fragments from the Fire: Poems.* 1993
0-933087-29-2 $8.95
Larry Smith. *Beyond Rust: Stories.* 1996
0-933087-39-X $9.95
Getting By: Stories of Working Lives. 1996
eds. David Shevin and Larry Smith 0-933087-41-1 $10.95
Human Landscapes: Three Books of Poems. 1997
(Includes Daniel Smith, Edwina Pendarvis, Philip St. Clair)
0-933087-42-X $10.95
Richard Hague. *Milltown Natural: Essays and Stories from a Life.* 1997
0-933087-44-6 $16.95 (cloth)
Maj Ragain. *Burley One Dark Sucker Fired: Poems.* 1998
0-933087-45-4 $9.95
Brooding the Heartlands: Poets of the Midwest, ed. M.L.Liebler. 1998
0-933087-50-0 $9.95
Writing Work: Writers on Working-Class Writing. 1999
eds. David Shevin, Larry Smith, Janet Zandy 0-933087-52-7 $10.95
Jim Ray Daniels. *No Pets: Stories.* 1999
0-933087-54-3 $10.95
Jeanne Bryner. *Blind Horse: Poems.* 1999
0-933087-57-8 $9.95
Naton Leslie. *Moving to Find Work: Poems.* 2000
0-933087-61-6 $9.95
David Kherdian. *The Neighborhood Years: Poems.* 2000
0-933087-62-4 $9.95
Our Working Lives: Short Stories of People and Work. 2000
eds. Bonnie Jo Campbell and Larry Smith
0-933087-63-2 $12.95
Allen Frost. *Ohio Trio: Fictions.* 2001
0-933087-68-3 $10.95
David Shevin. *Three Miles from Luckey: Poems.* 2002
0-933087-74-8 $10.95
Michael Salinger. *Neon: Stories & Poems.* 2002
0-933087-72.1 $10.95
*Working Hard for the Money:
America's Working Poor in Stories, Poems, and Photos.* 2002
eds. Mary E. Weems and Larry Smith
0-933087-77-2 $12.95